101 THINGS TO DO

Published by Lagoon Books
UK: PO Box 58528, London SW13 3AY
USA: 10685-B Hazelhust Dr. #9988
Houston, TX77043

Printed in China

ISBN: 978-190-2-81398-1

www.thelagoongroup.com

101 THINGS TO DO

#01 BAKE A CAKE

Budget: $$$ Time: ◷◷◷◷◷

There's nothing better than the smell of a cake baking in the oven, except perhaps for the moment when you actually taste it!

Making a cake is easy. All you need is a baking tin and a few inexpensive ingredients. Then, it's just a matter of measuring them out, mixing them in the right order, putting your cake in the oven, and remembering to take it out before it burns!

Here's an easy chocolate cake recipe to start you off:

Ingredients

For the cake
3/4 cup unsalted butter (at room temperature)
3/4 cup unsweetened cocoa powder
3/4 cup flour
1/4 teaspoon salt
1/2 teaspoon baking powder
1 cup sugar
3 eggs
1 teaspoon vanilla extract
1/2 cup buttermilk or sour cream

For the icing
2 cups confectioners' sugar
1/2 cup unsweetened cocoa powder
6 tablespoons unsalted butter (room temperature)
1/4 cup milk
1 teaspoon vanilla extract

Method

1. Preheat your oven to 350°F (180°C). Grease your baking tin with butter or cooking spray, so that the cake won't stick to it.

2. Mix the butter, eggs, vanilla extract, sugar, and buttermilk in a bowl. Use a whisk or a hand-mixer to blend the ingredients well.

3. Mix the flour, salt, cocoa powder, and baking powder in another small bowl. Stir them together until they are well incorporated.

4. Now add the dry mixture to the wet mixture. Mix thoroughly so that no white lumps of flour remain. You now have your cake batter.

5. Pour the batter into the baking tin. Use a spoon or spatula to scrape the sides of the bowl, so every bit of batter makes it into the tin.

6. Put the tin in the oven and bake for 30 minutes. Check the cake's progress every so often to ensure it doesn't burn. The cake is ready when a fork inserted into it comes out clean rather than coated with batter.

7. Take the cake from the oven. Set it on the worktop and let it cool for about 5 minutes before handling it.

8. Turn the cake out onto a plate. Use whatever plate you're planning on using to serve it.

9. Let the cake cool completely before frosting. If you try to add frosting to the cake while it's still warm, the frosting will melt and run off the sides. When the cake is cool and ready to frost, mix together the ingredients for the icing. Then use a knife to spread the mixture evenly over the cake.

10. Cut the cake into slices, and enjoy with a nice cup of tea or coffee!

There are lots more cake recipes you can find online.
Try http://www.joyofbaking.com/cakes.html for starters!

#02 START A BLOG

| Budget: $$$ | Time: 🕐🕐🕐🕐🕐 |

Set up your own blog and tell the world what you think about the issues of the day, or just what you had for lunch!

A blog is basically just an online diary. There is no need for any technical expertize, as there are various free blogging 'platforms' you can use. These provide the software to run your blog, and often web space on which to host it too. You can literally set up a blog in ten minutes or less.

The most popular free blogging platform is Blogger.com, which is owned by the world's favorite search engine, Google. Here's how to set up a Blogger blog in just ten minutes:

1. Go to www.blogger.com

2. Click on 'Create Your Blog Now'.

3. You will be asked to create a free Google account if you don't have one already.

4. Click on Continue and you'll be asked to choose a name and URL (web address) for your blog. For the name you can choose anything you like, but it's best to keep it short and sweet.

5. Choosing a URL is only a little more complicated. Blogger URLs take the form http://yourchoice.blogspot.com, where 'yourchoice' is the bit you choose yourself. Again in theory you can pick anything you like – but remember that many have already been taken, so you may need to be a bit creative to get your URL accepted. You can always use hyphens and even underscores.

6. Once you have chosen your blog's name and URL, click to continue again and you will be taken to a page where you can choose your blog's theme (design/color scheme). A wide range of choices are available, so pick any you like the look of. You can always change it later if you have second thoughts.

7. After waiting a few moments, you should see a message that says your blog has been created. Congratulations, you're a blogger! Now click on the 'Start Posting' arrow and get to work!

You can even make money as a blogger!

For example, from your Blogger.com control panel you can sign up for the Google AdSense advertising program. Once you're registered, adverts automatically appear on the side of your blog's page . Any time someone clicks on one of these you will receive a share of the fee paid by the advertizer.

#03 PUBLISH YOUR OWN EBOOK

Budget: $$$ Time: 🕐🕐🕐🕑🕐

They say everyone has a book inside them. Well, why not release the one in you!

Until recently, publishing your own book was a major undertaking and expensive too, but the rise of ebooks has changed all that.

In particular, the huge popularity of Amazon's Kindle device (and rival ebook readers such as the Kobo and the Nook) means that more ebooks are sold nowadays than traditional ones. And Amazon has made it easy for anyone to publish and sell their own ebook by means of Kindle Direct Publishing (KDP for short).

Publishing a Kindle ebook is a simple process. Essentially, all you have to do is write your book in Microsoft Word, save it in HTML (web) format, and upload it via the Amazon KDP website at https://kdp.amazon.com.

Unlike traditional books, Kindle ebooks can be as short as a few thousand words, so there's no need to create an epic. You can write fiction or nonfiction as you like. Spend a little time browsing the Kindle Store and this should give you plenty of ideas.

Once your Kindle ebook is published, anyone will be able to purchase it from Amazon. You can set your own price, and you will then receive a royalty of up to 70 per cent on sales. That compares well with the measly 10 percent typically paid to print authors.

Amazon has plenty more advice for would-be ebook authors on the KDP website, and they also have a free ebook titled Building Your Book for Kindle which you can download from the online store (just search for the ID B007URVZJ6).

<u>More Tips</u>

• Keep the formatting as simple as possible. Complex layouts are unlikely to survive conversion to ebook format.

• Create an eye-catching description of your book for the Kindle Store. You're allowed to use up to 4,000 characters, so make the most of it. Check out the sales pages of some Kindle bestsellers for inspiration.

• Price your title between $2.99 and $9.99 – this will ensure you qualify to receive Amazon's highest (70 per cent) royalty rate. Books priced outside this range receive only the standard 35 per cent royalty.

• Make sure the first few pages of your ebook hook the reader. People can see the first 10 per cent of your book free in the store. If the opening pages don't grab them, they will soon move on to something else.

• Create an attractive cover image for your ebook. This can have a very persuasive effect on potential buyers browsing the site. You can use the KDP free cover maker tool, or try www.fiverr.com, where there are people offering to create ebook covers for just $5.

If you are very lucky (and/or talented) your book could become an Amazon bestseller and maybe even propel you into the growing ranks of Kindle millionaires. But if not, you will still have the satisfaction of being a published author in the world's favorite online bookstore!

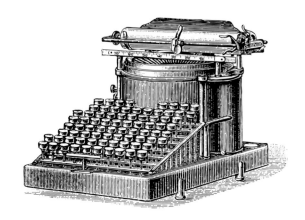

#04 LEARN TO JUGGLE

Budget: $$$ Time: 🕐🕐🕐🕐🕐

Not only is juggling fun, it's great for improving your concentration and relieving stress. It is also a pleasant form of light exercise, and is guaranteed to make you wow at any party!

Juggling is a skill anyone can learn at any age. While some folk have a greater natural aptitude than others, with enough practice anyone can learn the basic three-ball cascade (at least).

Most people find it easiest to start with special juggling balls, as these are comfortable to hold and don't bounce too much if you drop them. Juggling ball sets can be obtained from specialist stores, toy shops, and online stores such as Amazon.

Once you have your juggling balls, follow the three-step plan below:

1. Start with one ball and throw it from one hand to the other and back in a sidewise figure of eight pattern (see diagram below). Try not to look at your hands but focus on the top of the throw. This will help you learn to throw accurately.

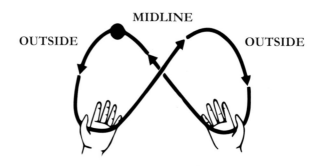

MIDLINE

OUTSIDE   OUTSIDE

2. Once you are comfortable doing this, add a second ball. Start with one in each hand, and when the first ball peaks throw the other one in the air and catch the first ball in the same hand. Once you can do this ten times in a row, move to step three.

3. Start with two balls in one hand and one in the other. Toss one ball from the hand holding two, and when it peaks throw the single ball in your other hand. As this one peaks, throw the other ball from the hand that held two originally. Keep going, catching and throwing alternately from one hand and then the other. Congratulations, you're juggling!

More Tips

• Ensure that the balls stay in a vertical plane in front of you. A common mistake is to throw them forwards. If you find yourself doing this, try practicing in front of a wall.

• Don't beat yourself up about dropping balls. It's an inevitable part of the learning process.

• Throw using your elbow, not your wrist or shoulder. Try to keep your elbows quite close to your sides.

• If you really can't get the hang of juggling with balls, try beanbags or even scarves. These are slower-moving than juggling balls, and can make it easier to grasp the sequence of moves required.

• For additional inspiration, check out the animated three-ball juggling lessons at www.wikihow.com/Juggle.

#05 SET UP A BOOK CLUB

Budget: $$$ Time: 🕐🕐🕐🕐🕐

Many people find that joining a book club is great for getting them back in the reading habit. And beyond that, it can be a lot of fun as well. Refreshments are usually provided, and the conversations can range well beyond the book under discussion!

Here's a step-by-step guide to setting up a book club:

1. Start with a few friends or colleagues, then gradually add new members. Use local noticeboards, or social networks such as Facebook and Twitter to spread the word.

2. As a rough guide, aim for six to ten people initially. Fewer than this and it can be hard to get a discussion started. Too many, and shyer people may not get heard.

3. Agree a venue for your first meeting. Many book clubs meet in members' homes, but others meet in libraries, bookstores, social clubs, and even bars and restaurants (as long as they aren't too noisy).

4. At the first meeting establish some ground rules. These should include what time the group will meet, how books will be chosen, who will host, and who will lead discussions. You need to decide whether there will be any restrictions on the type of book (e.g. just fiction, just modern books). You should also set a schedule for the first few months.

5. Continue to meet, and invite new members when the opportunity arises. Don't be disappointed if a few people drop out – changing commitments and priorities make this inevitable. View it as an opportunity to bring fresh faces into the group.

<u>More Tips</u>

• Choose books that are easy and affordable for members to buy (or borrow). Check out the best-seller lists for inspiration, or spend a little time browsing the Goodreads.com website.

• A rule that works well for many book clubs is that whoever will be acting as host/hostess for the meeting gets to choose what book members will read.

• It's not essential, but having refreshments can undoubtedly help the discussion to flow. At the very least, have tea or coffee available and a few snacks. It may be best to avoid alcoholic drinks, though!

• If you're leading the discussion, prepare some questions in advance to ask members. This can prime the pump, after which discussion will hopefully flow freely. All members should bring notes of any points they want to share at the meeting.

For anyone who enjoys reading, starting or joining a book club has many attractions. Reading is a solitary pastime, but when a book has moved or stimulated you it's great to be able to share this with other people.

In addition, a group encourages you to think more deeply about the books you read, and why you like some and hate others. Many people find that belonging to a book group greatly enhances their enjoyment of reading generally.

#06 GO TO THE END OF THE LINE

Budget: $$$ Time: 🕐🕐🕑🕐🕐

Is there a bus, train or subway route you use regularly? One day when you have some free time, get a ticket to the last stop on the line (or if that's too far, another stop you have never visited before).

Take a camera with you and a notebook (or a device such as a smartphone that can be used for both purposes). Spend a few hours wandering around the place in question. Keep an open mind and try to see everything with fresh, curious eyes, almost as if you were a visitor from another planet.

Take some photos and make notes on your discoveries, especially anything that intrigues or puzzles you. Ask yourself some questions such as:

• What do they make at that factory?
• What is the story behind that street name?
• What is the history of that now-derelict church?
• What is that stream or river, and where does it go?
• What is the unusual tree growing in that garden?
• Whom does that statue portray (and why?)
• What crops do they grow at that farm?
• What is that large new building going to be used for?

If there are people around who look local (and not too busy), take the chance to ask them some of your questions. Most people are delighted to answer questions about their hometown, especially if it's not a typical tourist destination!

When you get home, do some additional online research about the area. In particular, see if you can find answers to the questions you weren't able to answer while you were there.

Through this exercise you can discover some fascinating places you never knew existed before. You will also get some fresh air and exercise, and have a chance to practice your internet research skills!

Once you have done this, you may well find there are questions you can only answer by revisiting the place concerned. Or through your research you may unearth other interesting features you missed on your first visit. Either way, you may then wish to plan a return visit at your leisure.

Alternatively, why not try visiting other destinations along the line that are unfamiliar to you as well? Even the unlikeliest places may have aspects that you want to learn more about.

Try this with your own hometown as well. Approach it with fresh eyes and you may discover some unsuspected gems on your own doorstep.

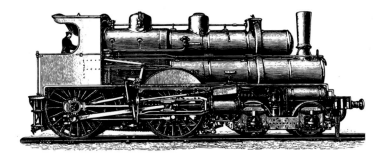

#07 HOLD A PAPER PLANE
COMPETITION

Budget: $$$ Time: 🕐🕐🕐🕐🕐

Who doesn't enjoy making and flying paper planes? This activity is fun for all the family, and a great alternative to boring telly.

To make a basic paper dart, follow the step-by-step instructions below:

1. Fold a single sheet of paper in half lengthwise, and run your thumbnail along the fold to crease it sharply. Then unfold the paper again.

2. Fold down the top corners, as shown by the arrows.

3. Fold over the edges towards the center line again.

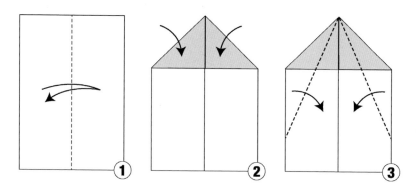

4. Fold the two sides together along the center line.

5. Create a wing crease from near the front to the back of the plane and fold the wings down.

6. If the plane has a tendency to nosedive, try folding up the rear end of the wings slightly to provide extra lift.

Once everyone has completed their planes, it's time for them to compete.

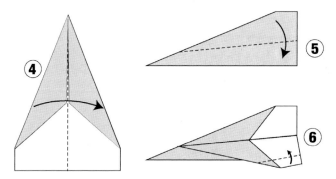

Ideally, it's best to go out in the garden or a nearby park, but if the weather doesn't allow this, a long hallway or living room should be fine. Alternatively, if you have access to a sports hall or similar, that would be perfect.

Get everyone to throw their plane from the same point and see whose travels the furthest. To make it even more fun, you could award points (e.g. 5 for first place, 4 for second, 3 for third, and so on) and have multiple rounds. Have five rounds, say, and see whose plane scores the most points overall.

• Try experimenting with plane designs to see if you can gain an advantage this way. Various alternative designs can be found online at www.wikihow. com/Make-a-Paper-Airplane, www.amazingpaperairplanes.com, and www. paperaeroplanes.com.

• You can also try creating your own design, but to keep it fair for everyone follow these three simple rules: (1) use only a single sheet of paper, (2) no additional materials (paperclips, staples, glue, tape, etc) may be used, and (3) the paper must not be cut or torn.

• For even more fun use colored paper, and/or decorate your plane using bright, gel-ink pens.

#08 CREATE A
HANGING BASKET

Budget: $$$ Time: 🕐🕐🕐🕐🕐

Hanging baskets can make any home more attractive. Ready-made baskets can be expensive, so why not save some money by creating your own?

You can also choose whatever flowers you like to put in, and should end up with something much more attractive and to your taste than anything you could ever buy in a shop. Here's an easy, step-by-step guide to creating a beautiful hanging basket to put up outside your home:

1. Choose a basket from a garden center or hardware store. The main options are solid plastic, ceramic or wire mesh.

2. Line the basket. This will help keep the soil in place and reduce the need for watering. The best lining for a hanging basket is sphagnum moss. This works especially well with hanging baskets that are wire based. An alternative is polythene. Punch some holes in the base of this to allow water to seep through and ensure good drainage.

3. Add soil. A good-quality potting mix or compost should be used. Add a slow-release fertilizer to this, and mix well before filling the basket.

4. Pick strong plants that are appropriate for growing in a basket. It's best to use established plants that are either flowering or close to flowering. Arrange large plants first and tuck in smaller plants around them, with trailing plants around the sides. A wide variety of plants work well in hanging baskets. They include Lobelia, Nasturtiums, Begonias, Pansies, Polyanthus, Fuchsias, Verbena, Petunias and Impatiens ('Busy Lizzies').

5. Choose a location to display the basket to best effect. Try to avoid full sunshine or full shade though, as few plants can withstand this if they are growing in baskets.

6. Hang the basket carefully. Once filled with soil and plants it will be heavy, and it will become even heavier when you water it. Take care when putting it up (ideally this is a two-person job). Use a step-ladder placed on a flat surface to ensure it won't wobble. Make sure the hook used to suspend the basket is strong and securely fitted.

7. Water your basket regularly. During hot weather you may need to water daily to stop it drying out completely. Even if (as recommended) you have used a slow-release fertilizer in the soil, it can still be a good idea to add a liquid fertilizer as well as the season progresses.

8. Pinch off any flower heads that are past their best to keep your basket looking fresh.

Follow these simple steps and you will soon have a stunning display that lasts all summer long and makes your home the envy of your neighbors!

#09 PLAY A ■ ■ ■ BOARD GAME

Budget: $$$ Time: 🕐🕐🕐🕐🕐

Board games are great for bringing the whole family together – and of course friends and neighbors are welcome to join in as well!

Board games are inexpensive and can provide many hours of entertainment. They may be purchased from toy shops, stationery stores, and online. Here are a few of the most popular options:

Monopoly – This classic property-trading board game dates back to the Great Depression of the 1930s. Buy streets and put up houses and hotels, then charge your fellow players exorbitant rents and drive them bankrupt. Fun for all the family!

Risk – This board game is all about military strategy. It is played on a map of the Earth, which is divided into 42 territories. The aim is to defeat your rival armies, conquer territories, and ultimately take over the world.

Cluedo – Bring out your inner Sherlock with this brain-stretching game of memory and deduction. The murderer was Mrs. White, in the kitchen, with a candlestick holder!

Trivial Pursuit – Everyone enjoys showing off their knowledge in a quiz game, and Trivial Pursuit is still one of the best. Players have to go around the board answering questions in one of six color-coded categories. Once they have collected a 'wedge' for each category, they must go to the center and answer a question in a category chosen by the other players. The first to answer correctly wins.

Scrabble – Another classic. If you enjoy word games, this one is right up your street. Aim to make high-scoring words from the letters you draw, and avoid being left with X, Q and J at the end. Be sure to have a dictionary on hand to settle any disputes.

Game of Life – This modern board game lets you live the life of your dreams, but with many decisions to be made along the way. Will you go to college and get into debt, or go straight into the world of work? And will you chase the big money in the city or quality of life on the beach? Whoever has the most money and stamps in their passport at the end is the winner!

Alternatively, why not create your own board game? Get a large piece of plain card or even paper to use as the board and draw a route around it with spaces to land on. Put forfeits on some spaces, e.g. miss a turn, go back two spaces, impersonate a dying fly, and so on. All you need then are counters for playing pieces and dice to get round. You can have hours of fun making your game before you even start playing it!

More Tips

• Don't get too competitive – board games are meant to be fun!

• Ensure everyone understands the rules from the start.

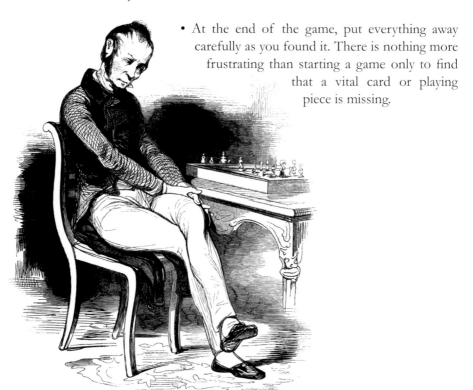

• At the end of the game, put everything away carefully as you found it. There is nothing more frustrating than starting a game only to find that a vital card or playing piece is missing.

#10 TAKE UP
STAR GAZING

Budget: $$$ Time: 🕐🕐🕐🕐🕐

Star gazing is a fascinating pastime, and you don't need to spend a single penny to get started.

Here's a step-by-step guide for your first star-gazing expedition:

1. Choose a clear night when no rain or storms are forecast. Dress suitably, with an extra sweater and/or blanket in case it gets cold later.

2. Prepare by reading some introductory textbooks, and take them with you on the night, together with star charts so you know what you are looking at (and for). Bring a torch as well so you can easily read them.

3. Invite friends or family members for company and to share your observations with. If you're planning on staying out for a while, it's a good idea to take a thermos with a hot drink and a few snacks.

4. Choose an open area without too many trees or buildings to block your view. Try also to avoid places with too many electric lights nearby. These cause 'sky glow', also known as light pollution, which reduces the visibility of many of the fascinating things to be seen in the night sky.

5. Contrary to what you might think, there's no need for a telescope – there are lots of interesting things you can observe with the naked eye. If you want to see more, a pair of binoculars would be a good choice. They allow more light to enter your eyes, making dimmer objects easier to see, while still maintaining a wide view of the sky. Binoculars are also light and portable, less expensive than astronomical telescopes, and don't require setting up.

6. Start by identifying some of the main constellations, stars and planets. A good starting point is The Big Dipper, also known as The Plough. This pan-shaped cluster has seven of the brightest stars in the sky. Once you have found it, follow the line of the two stars at the end of the pan to Polaris, otherwise known as the North Star (see picture below).

More Tips

• If you want to get higher magnifications than offered by binoculars, you may want to think about buying a telescope. There are many astronomical phenomena that can only be seen clearly through a telescope, including distant galaxies and even some of the planets. Take your time selecting a telescope, as there are many factors to consider, including cost, portability, magnification, and so on.

• If you have a smartphone, there are various free and low-cost apps that will help with your star gazing. Typically these 'augmented reality' apps re-create the night sky based on your GPS coordinates. Point your device upward and it will reveal exactly what you are looking at. These astronomy apps are a massive boon for star gazers.

• There are many excellent free websites that will help you deepen your knowledge of star gazing and astronomy. For starters, try www.space.com, www.skyandtelescope.com, and http://stardate.org/nightsky.

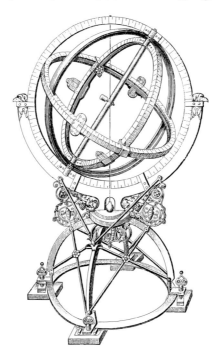

#11 GO
RUNNING

Budget: $$$ Time: 🕐🕐🕐🕐🕐

Running is a healthy activity almost anyone can do. It will boost your physique, ward off stress, and help you lose weight by burning off calories.

What's more, runners may live longer and stay healthier. Researchers at Stanford University found that regular runners have a 39 per cent lower risk of dying an early death compared with healthy non-runners of the same age.

So, taking up running has a lot to recommend it. But before you start pounding the pavements, to minimize the risk of injury, it's important to prepare properly. In particular, ensure that you have the right kit.

Most important is a well-fitting pair of running shoes. These will feel light and comfortable and help you avoid blisters or worse. It's best to buy your shoes from a dedicated sports shoe store. The staff there will be able to measure your feet accurately and recommend the best shoes for you.

In addition, to avoid pain, women should invest in a good-quality sports bra. Before you start any run, warm up with some gentle stretches for five to ten minutes. You should always end your run with a cool-down as well.

Especially if you haven't done any exercise for a while, it's important to build up gradually. Follow the week-by-week plan below:

Weekly Plan
Each week, try to fit in three sessions of the activity.

Week 1 – Walk for six minutes, then jog at an easy pace for one. Repeat three times.

Week 2 – Walk for five minutes, then jog for two. Repeat three times.

Week 3 – Walk for three minutes, then jog for four. Repeat four times.

Week 4 – Walk for two minutes, then jog for five. Repeat four times.

Week 5 – Walk for two minutes, then jog for eight. Repeat three times.

Week 6 – Walk for two minutes, then jog for nine. Repeat three times.

Week 7 – Walk for one minute, then jog for eleven. Repeat three times.

Week 8 – For your first run this week, try walking for five minutes at the start and end, and run for 20 minutes in between. By the end of the week, try to run for 30 minutes without stopping.

Aim to run for 30 minutes three times a week, and you'll notice that your stamina and fitness will continue to improve. Soon you'll be ready for your first 10K!

<u>More Tips</u>

• Drink some water at the end of every run (and in the middle of longer runs). It's important to replace the fluid you lose during the run as soon as possible.

• Change your running shoes regularly – most experts recommend getting a new pair every 500 miles.

• Rest after running to allow your muscle tissue to recover. When you first start your running program, it's a good idea to schedule at least one day of rest between runs.

#12 BECOME A VOLUNTEER

Budget: $$$ Time: ⏱⏱⏱⏱⏱

Why not donate a little of your time to a local charity or other good cause. Not only will this benefit your local community, you'll be meeting new people and acquiring new skills and experiences that you can add to your résumé.

Wherever you live, whatever your age or background, there will be organizations that can make good use of your services. The possibilities range from assisting at a local school or youth group to becoming a volunteer tourist guide. Some other options include:

- driving
- office work
- counseling (phone or face to face)
- shop work
- play schemes and summer camps
- gardening and environmental work
- assisting at sporting events
- working with elderly people
- hospital volunteering
- helping out at a local theater or concert hall
- sharing your creative talents
- political canvassing
- writing and social media work
- public speaking
- litter-picking
- fundraising
- and many more!

Many towns and cities have a volunteer center or similar organization that acts as a local clearing house. Pay them a visit and let them know the sorts of work you are interested in, and the skills and experience you have to offer. They should be able to suggest several local nonprofit organizations that would be delighted to hear from you.

Volunteering need not be a massive commitment. If all you want to do is a couple of hours a week, that will still be much appreciated. Just be sure to discuss this in advance and agree a schedule that suits both you and the organization you will be working with. If the work will involve any out-of-pocket expenditure (e.g. travel costs) ask if they will be willing to reimburse this. It is also a good idea to find out if any training will be provided.

#13 PLAN A VACATION

Budget: $$$　　　　**Time: ◷◷◷◷◷**

Everybody needs a break, and planning a vacation can be almost as much fun as going, especially if you get all the family involved.

Nowadays there are lots of options for vacations, and you don't have to spend a fortune either. Here are a few possibilities to set you thinking…

Seaside – Sun, sea and sand – what's not to like? You could head for your nearest resort, or jet off somewhere more exotic. You could stay at a hotel or book a self-catering apartment.

Cruise – Cruises are fun for all ages and can be excellent value for money too. Many are all-inclusive, so once you're on board you don't have to open your wallet. There are different places to see every day, great food to eat, and most ships put on high-quality entertainment as well. As well as sea and island cruises, a growing range of river cruises are on offer.

City Break – Spend a weekend or longer in a city you have always wanted to visit. Check out the historic sites, hit the museums and galleries, take in a show, enjoy fine dining at a swanky restaurant, or simply shop till you drop!

Camping – Get back to nature with a few days in the country. You could take a tent, or go more upmarket with a caravan or motorhome. Take a camera and binoculars, and keep an eye out for the local wildlife.

Winter Sports – For the more energetic, a skiing or snowboarding vacation may be just the ticket. Most resorts offer tuition for complete beginners, and you can borrow all the kit you need if you're not sure whether the sport will be for you.

#14 MAKE YOUR OWN ICE CREAM

Budget: $$$　　　　Time: 🕐🕐🕑🕐🕐

Who doesn't like ice cream on a hot day?! Making your own is easy, and it's a great project if you have children.

You will get the best results if you have an ice-cream making machine, but you can still make it even if you don't. The recipe below will make a quart of ice cream, so double the quantities if you want more.

1. Mix up the following ingredients in a saucepan:

• 2 cups cream
• 1 cup whole milk
• 2/3 cup sugar
• 1 teaspoon vanilla extract
Optional: 1/2 cup cocoa powder for chocolate ice cream

2. Place the saucepan over medium/high heat and heat the mixture, stirring constantly, until the sugar dissolves completely.

3. Pour the cream base into a bowl, cover it, and place it in the refrigerator to cool down for an hour or two.

4. Pour the chilled base into your ice-cream maker and freeze according to the manufacturer's instructions. Depending on the type of machine you have, this might take one or more hours.

5. When the ice cream is partly frozen, add your favorite mix-ins to flavor it. A vanilla base tastes great with almost any type of fruit, candy or nut. Add around a cup of one or more of the following:

Sliced strawberries	Chopped chocolate bar	Peanut butter
Blackcurrants	Chopped candy bar	Candied pecans
Chopped cherries	Butterscotch chips	Chopped pistachios
Chopped peaches	Shredded coconut	

6. Turn the ice-cream maker back on to finish the freezing process, then put the ice cream in the freezer for about three hours. Enjoy your ice cream once it's frozen solid and creamy.

Making Ice Cream Without a Machine

For this quick and simple method you will need one quart-sized zip-top bag and one sandwich-sized zip-top bag. You will also need a cup of ordinary cooking salt and two cups of ice. Then follow the simple recipe below:

1. Combine half a cup of cream or whole milk, a tablespoon of sugar and a teaspoon of vanilla extract in a mixing bowl. Pour this into the sandwich-sized zip-top bag and seal it tightly.

2. Add the ice and salt to the large bag, and then place the smaller bag inside the larger one and seal it tightly as well.

3. Now shake the bag as hard as you can without bursting it, until the contents have the consistency of ice cream. This is likely to take five to ten minutes. You can hold the bag in a dish towel to stop your hands getting too cold.

4. Carefully open the large bag and take the small bag out. Open, pour out, and enjoy your ice cream!

Again, you can add fruit, or other ingredients if you wish, either at the start or the end. This method makes a single serving of ice cream, but of course it's easy to give everyone their own bags and ingredients and let them make their own portion!

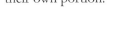

#15 GO SEE A BAND

Budget: $$$ Time: 🕐🕐🕐🕐🕐

When did you last see any live music? If it's been a while, why not check out who's on locally and book yourself a ticket?

There are lots of options according to your musical tastes. You might prefer pop or rock music, jazz, blues, country and western, folk, or even gospel. Different clubs and venues specialize in all of these genres. Or if your tastes are a little more traditional, a classical or choral music concert may appeal.

Another very popular option nowadays is a tribute band or singer. Some amazingly talented musicians perform in tribute acts, and you can enjoy the music at a fraction of what it would cost to see the stars themselves (assuming they are even around anymore).

You may also be able to take in some live music free of charge. Many pubs, bars and restaurants feature live music at the weekend. The musicians are unlikely to be household names, but you can still enjoy their sounds along with a drink and maybe a meal.

More Tips

• If there's a tourist information office in your town, go and pick up any leaflets they have.

• Get on the mailing lists of all the local concert venues, and check out their websites as well.

• Ask your music-loving friends if they have seen any good bands recently and if they know of any good concerts coming up.

• If you have a favorite band you would like to see, check out their Facebook page and/or website to see if they are performing anywhere near you.

• Concert tickets can be pricey, so see if there are any discounts you may be eligible for. Some venues also offer lower-priced tickets on the night, or for seats with restricted visibility.

• Dress appropriately for the weather, but assume the interior of the venue will become quite warm. Dress in layers, and consider a light jacket if it's cold.

• Keep your ticket on you at all times. Should you leave your seat for any reason you may be asked to show your ticket to return.

• Try to eat before you go, as the food at concert venues is often poor quality or very expensive.

• Aim to arrive early to get a good seat if they aren't pre-allocated. This is also a good time to check out the merchandise, before all the best stuff is sold.

• Be patient when leaving, as lots of other people may be departing at the same time. If there are traffic marshals, follow their advice and instructions.

Seeing good music performed live really is better than listening to any recording or watching it on TV. Enjoy the show!

#16 PLANT YOUR OWN HERB GARDEN

Budget: $$$ Time: 🕐🕐🕐🕐🕐

What could be nicer than growing your own herbs and adding them to your favorite recipes? Not only can you save a lot of money this way, the herbs will be fresher and tastier than anything you can buy from the shops.

You only need a few square feet of ground to grow herbs, but if you don't have even that you can still grow them in a container, or even pots on your window sill. Pick a spot near the kitchen, so you can step out and snip off a sprig without having to hike across the yard.

You can grow most herbs from seed, but it can be quicker and easier to buy small plants from garden centers or farmers' markets.

Here are some of the best herbs to start with:

Basil – This is among the easiest herbs to grow. Just remember to water it regularly and cut leaves from the top rather than the sides.

Mint – There are many varieties of mint, and most grow vigorously. Indeed, you may need to cut your mint back regularly to stop it squeezing out other herbs.

Chives – Chives are also easy to grow. They have a delicate onion flavor. Cut them back after they flower to encourage fresh growth.

Dill – This pretty, yellow-flowered herb grows best in sunny spots. Its tangy leaves and seeds are great for all sorts of culinary purposes.

Oregano – This versatile herb grows well even in poor soil. It is a staple in Mediterranean cookery.

Rosemary – This evergreen shrub prefers a hot, dry environment. It's great on pizza and focaccia bread, and also goes very well with potatoes!

Thyme – This Greek herb loves heat and sun, and is a magnet for honeybees. It is among the most versatile of all herbs, going well with red meat, fish and poultry, as well as rice and vegetable dishes.

Parsley – This is another versatile herb. It will grow quite happily in shady conditions. It is popular as a garnish and breath freshener, but goes well in many recipes too. It is also said to have health and medicinal benefits.

<u>More Tips</u>

• If the soil in your garden is poor quality, add fertilizer to improve it. If you are growing in pots or containers, a good-quality potting compost should be used.

• Give each plant enough space. If you crowd them together they won't grow as well.

• If using containers, ensure they are well-drained. Water regularly, but not so much that the roots become waterlogged.

• Give plants growing in pots or containers a liquid fertilizer monthly. This will encourage vigorous growth.

• Snip off leaves – don't tear them. Harvest your herbs regularly, as this encourages them to keep producing new growth.

• Pinch off any tips or flowers that appear. Once a herb produces flowers, it's trying to end its life-cycle.

Finally, having gone to the trouble of growing your own herbs, don't forget to seek out some delicious recipes in which to use them!

#17 TRY STREET PHOTOGRAPHY

Budget: $$$ **Time: ◷◷◷◷◷**

You don't need to visit exotic locations to take great photos, and you certainly don't need a top-of-the-range camera.

The very familiarity of your home town or city can mean that it's easy to overlook the host of interesting images available on its streets. So why not charge up your camera and head out to see what photo opportunities you can find?

Here are four great project ideas to start you off:

Candid Portraits
In most countries if people are out in public it is perfectly legal to photograph them. If you use a long (telephoto) lens you can take pictures from a distance without your subjects even knowing you are doing so. But equally, if you spend some time getting to know someone before taking their picture, you may be able to get some even better images.

Macro Photographs
As with nature photography, even ordinary, familiar things can take on a new and surprising dimension when you photograph them up close. You will need a macro lens for your camera, or at least a camera with a macro setting.

Signs and Graffiti
Every town and city can provide these! Street art is often vibrant and colorful, and once you've found something you like it's just a matter of deciding how much background to show. Even ordinary street signs can take on a new (and sometimes humorous) significance when juxtaposed against other signs and objects.

Theme Your Photos

Try shooting pictures where a single color dominates the frame. Not only will this help you focus on looking for one type of subject, it will also make for a nice collection at the end. Alternatively, you could choose a location such as a market or railway station and try to capture all its many aspects through your photos.

<u>More Tips</u>

• Most modern smartphones can take great pictures as well. They also have the advantage that they won't attract undue attention.

• Take lots of photos – it's cheap and easy with modern digital cameras – and discard all but the best.

• It's not against the law to photograph children in public, but to avoid potential problems it's best to ask their parents' permission first.

• Study the work of successful street photographers for inspiration and to give you something to aim for. The website www.street-photographers. com has some great examples.

• When you have some photos you like, share them with others. At the very least you could create a Facebook album for friends and family to admire, or you could build a website or blog to display them to the world.

Street photography has many attractions for anyone with even just a passing interest in the visual arts. Not only that, it can give you fresh air and exercise, and open your eyes to the amazing variety of things going on in your home town or city. It might even prove to be the start of a life-long hobby or career.

#18 BOOK A HOT-AIR BALLOON RIDE

Budget: $$$ Time: 🕐🕐🕐🕐🕐

Going on a hot-air balloon ride is an adventure open to anyone of almost any age. Most people find it an exhilarating, even magical, experience.

You float high above the ground, with almost no sound but the occasional burst from the jets, and just the distant murmur of traffic drifting up from far below.

Wherever you live, the chances are that not far away is a ballooning company ready and waiting to transport you to the skies! Look in your local Yellow Pages for some possibilities, or search online.

Rides are typically an hour in duration, although you should allow three or four hours for the whole experience.

More Tips

• Rides normally take place in the early morning or at dusk, as this is when the winds tend to be at their calmest.

• Flights will only go ahead if the weather is suitable, so it is best to phone beforehand to ensure that yours hasn't been canceled. The pilot has to make a judgment on whether it is safe to launch. He will not do so if he thinks there would be any risk to passengers.

• There is no bathroom on a hot-air balloon, so be sure to take a 'comfort stop' before you embark.

• You get into the basket by climbing over the sides. Steps are provided, but nevertheless people with mobility difficulties may be excluded for health and safety reasons. Ask about this in advance if you are concerned.

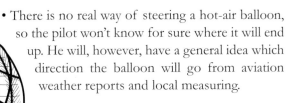

• There is no real way of steering a hot-air balloon, so the pilot won't know for sure where it will end up. He will, however, have a general idea which direction the balloon will go from aviation weather reports and local measuring.

• There is little sense of motion on a balloon flight, as the balloon simply follows the wind. Few people experience motion sickness on a balloon flight.

• Passengers may be expected to help roll up the balloon once it has landed and load it onto the chase vehicle that returns it (and them) to the departure point.

If you enjoy your balloon flight, you might want to consider buying one of your own. A good starting point for information would be a local ballooning club, or there might be a ballooning festival you could attend. Most balloon enthusiasts are delighted to talk about their hobby (or occupation) and will be happy to give you the benefit of their experience and recommendations.

Note that in most countries anyone wanting to pilot a hot-air balloon has to take a state-approved training course leading to a balloon pilot's license. They will be required to successfully complete written and practical examinations, and obtain a prescribed number of hours of instruction. Only after this will they be allowed to pilot a balloon.

#19 LEARN TO MEDITATE

Budget: $$$ Time: ⏰⏰⏰⏰⏰

In our fast-moving, often stressful, world, more and more people are discovering the benefits of meditation as a way to relax and get back in touch with themselves.

Here's a simple exercise in 'mindfulness' meditation you can try every morning to get your day off to the best possible start. It takes just ten minutes to do, and if you practice it regularly, it should bring you calmness and peace of mind. The technique is best used early in the day, but you can also use it any time you need to de-stress and relax.

Step 1 – Set aside ten minutes when you know you won't be interrupted. Find a quiet, comfortable place, and switch off your cell phone.

Step 2 – Sit or lie down, ensuring that your spine is straight. With your eyes closed, relax and focus on breathing gently through your nostrils. Become aware of how the air feels as it enters and leaves your body.

Step 3 – Allow your thoughts to come and go, without pursuing them. During this process you may become aware of ideas that you want to explore or solutions to problems, but just observe them and let them pass. Trust that these thoughts and ideas will still be there for you later. As your awareness turns inward, the stream of busy thoughts will slow to a trickle, and then stop.

Step 4 – Keep your mind focused on breathing slowly for up to ten minutes (you can use a timer if you like). Allow your body to relax fully, and your mind simply to observe what is going on, without trying to intervene in any way.

Step 5 – After the ten minutes are up, take a few deep breaths, open your eyes and – in your own time – get up and continue your day.

Hold the memory of your meditation in a corner of your mind and touch base with it throughout the day – maybe when you're on the bus or having your morning coffee. Find small moments to remind yourself how it felt to enjoy that calmness and mental clarity. You don't need to go through the whole process – just take a couple of deep breaths, and notice how you feel, and any areas of tension.

Mindfulness meditation is a powerful technique, bringing calmness and clarity of thought in just a few minutes. Some people find it difficult at first, but most improve with practice.

<u>More Tips</u>

• If you find meditating with your eyes closed difficult, try candle meditation instead. Focusing on the flame can make it easier to still your mind and resist distraction.

• Some people find they get more benefit from meditation if they do it with a friend or loved one. Just be sure you agree on the ground rules before you start!

• Don't stress! Meditation is meant to be a relaxing, pleasurable experience. No matter what happens during your meditation session, try not to become angry or self-critical. Be kind to yourself.

#20 TRY WHITE WATER RAFTING

Budget: $$$ Time: ⏰⏰⏰⏰⏰

White water rafting is an exciting, exhilarating activity, suitable for most people from about the age of six upwards. Participants guide and paddle a raft through white water, or a river's rapids. The sport's popularity began to grow when it became part of the Olympic Games in the 1970s.

White water rafting is great for families and groups of friends, and ideal for people who enjoy being outside or in the water. For the easiest runs you don't even need to be able to swim (although this is obviously a great skill to have).

Most white water rafting trips are group adventures in rented paddle rafts or oar rafts. Paddle rafts generally seat four to eight people and a guide. These inflatable, plastic rafts are quick in the water and may be taken out on any level of white water. Most commercial services use paddle rafts. Everyone is expected to paddle, while a guide positioned at the rear of the boat shouts out instructions.

Alternatively, if you're looking for a less strenuous experience, you could rent an oar raft. These are inflatable and powered by a guide with a set of long wooden oars. These rafts usually seat three to five people, and are taken on easy to moderate runs.

Either way, your first step will be to select a white water park or river that caters for beginners and book a trip with a professional guide or instructor. This is very important, as the guide will know the water well and be able to provide expert advice aimed at keeping you safe and helping you enjoy the whole experience.

Once you're in your raft, be sure that your life jacket is fastened securely before the raft starts to move. Ensure that your group is seated so that the weight is evenly distributed, and keep any young children near you at all times. Have fun, and enjoy the ride!

#21 MAKE YOUR OWN JAM

Budget: $$$ **Time: ⏰⏰⏰⏰⏰**

If you have a surfeit of fruit in your garden, making jam is a great way to use it up. But even if you don't, fresh fruit is often available to buy cheaply from shops and farmers' markets when in season.

Making your own jam is easy, and the aroma while preparing it is delightful. Home-made jam tastes fresher than any store-bought stuff, and it also makes a very welcome gift.

To start you off, here is a simple recipe for making fresh strawberry jam:

Ingredients

2 lbs fresh strawberries
1/4 cup lemon juice
4 cups white sugar

1. In a wide bowl, crush the strawberries in batches until you have four cups of mashed berries.

2. In a heavy bottomed saucepan, mix the strawberries, sugar and lemon juice. Stir over a low heat until the sugar is dissolved.

3. Increase the heat to high, and bring the mixture to a full rolling boil. Boil, stirring often, until the mixture reaches 220°F (105°C).

4. Transfer the jam to hot sterile jars, leaving 1/4 to 1/2 inch headspace, and seal.

5. Allow the jars to cool and store them in a refrigerator. Aim to eat home-made jam within a couple of months. Alternatively, it can be kept for longer in a freezer (use plastic containers or zip-top bags).

#22 GO FOR A WALK

Budget: $$$ Time: ⏰⏰⏰⏰⏰

Walking is an activity open to everyone, young and old. It's a pleasant form of light exercise, and you'll get some fresh air as well. Approached more seriously, it can also be a good way to lose weight and boost your overall health and fitness.

You can walk on your own or with friends, in the country or in the city. Walking alone can be great for de-stressing, while walking in a group can be an enjoyable sociable activity. During your walk you can talk about anything or everything, and if you're in a group it's easy to switch from chatting to one person to another.

You don't need much by way of kit, unless you plan to walk long distances or well off the beaten track. The most important thing is a well-fitting pair of boots that will support your feet and ankles. Thick woolen socks are good to wear with them, and waterproof clothing in case you get caught in a shower. A backpack is also invaluable for carrying food and drink, waterproofs, and any other items you might want to have with you (such as a map, camera or binoculars).

One other thing you could consider is walking poles. Serious walkers use these to provide rhythm to their pace and for added support. On flat, smooth terrain they aren't really necessary. But on less certain terrain, or steep slopes, they can give extra stability, and older people often turn to them for help with knee pain. Poles can also be useful as aids when climbing rocks or boulders, and to probe the depth of mud or water.

Starting Your Own Social Walking Group

If you enjoy walking, why not take it a step further and start your own social walking group? These are popular among people of all ages. Groups typically meet once a week to walk a route that has been decided in advance.

Many walking groups are composed of people who work or study together, or belong to a particular club, church or other social group. But there is nothing to prevent you starting a walking group with friends and family, and then growing it by word of mouth.

Social walks often end at a pub, bar or restaurant, so frequently the social aspect will continue over drinks or a meal. If you are new to an area, starting (or joining) a walking group can be a great way of meeting new friends. They are also very popular with older people, who appreciate both the company and the light exercise.

More Tips

• Do a bit of light stretching to warm up before the start.

• Wear some light-colored clothing to ensure you are clearly visible to drivers.

• When walking alone always let someone know where you're going and your expected time of return.

• In hot weather wear a hat and sunglasses, and use sun block on any exposed skin.

• Take some water with you and sip it regularly to avoid getting dehydrated.

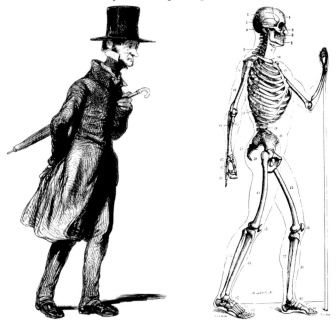

#23 LEARN TO PLAY THE PIANO

Budget: $$$ Time: ○○○○○

The piano is a wonderfully versatile instrument. Anyone can learn to play a few tunes on it, but fully mastering its potential can be a lifetime's challenge.

If you want to learn the piano, it's best if you can get an instrument of your own. Practice is the key to learning and improving, and having your own piano will allow you to practice at any time to suit yourself.

If there really is no alternative, you can use a good-quality electronic keyboard instead, but this is not recommended. You will have more trouble learning proper posture and hand positioning than you would with an actual piano, and you will never be able to exert as much control over the sound it creates.

Once you have obtained your piano, your first step should be to get it tuned and examined by a professional. After that, you will need a bench and some music to play. It's best to buy an adjustable piano bench, as this will allow you to set the height that is most comfortable for you.

Ask your local music store for recommendations on basic, easy-to-play piano music books. It's likely they will be able to suggest at least a couple you can use. If possible, get one book that contains advice for complete beginners and includes scales and arpeggios, and one book with simple, complete songs to practice, such as old folk songs.

You may also, of course, wish to pay for lessons from a piano teacher. These will usually take place at their home or studio, though some teachers also visit students in their own homes. Lessons typically take an hour or so. Before signing up with a piano teacher, check their qualifications and ask if you can speak to some of their current or former students.

#24 LEARN TO DRAW CARTOONS

Budget: $$$ Time: 🕐🕐🕐🕐🕐

Drawing cartoons is great fun, and there's no need to be an expert artist either! Cartoons are basically just simplified versions of things we see in real life.

Most cartoon characters begin with a few basic shapes – squares, circles, triangles and so on. These are put together to create a framework for the cartoon. The cartoonist then draws around and over this to create a recognizable character, and (optionally) finishes by coloring it in.

All you really need to get started as a cartoonist is a pencil or marker pen and some plain paper. Alternatively, if you prefer to work on a computer, you could use a tablet and stylus.

There are a number of good introductory books on cartooning. The Big Book of Cartooning by Bruce Blitz is one popular choice and Humongous Book of Cartooning by Christopher Hart is another. Both these authors are working professional cartoonists themselves, and they share hundreds of helpful tips and ideas in their books.

As you might expect, there is also plenty of advice and instruction for would-be cartoonists online. At www.how-to-draw-cartoons-online.com there are free lessons on everything from how to draw cartoon aliens to drawing characters, landscapes and clothes. Within each category there are some lessons at beginner level, some at intermediate, and some at advanced. And, of course, all the lessons are fully illustrated, with examples.

As with most skills, the key to success with cartooning is practice – the more you do it, the better you will become. It is also a good idea to focus on one particular type of cartoon first – e.g. cartoon men or animals – and keep working on this until you are good at it. After that, you can move on to other types of cartoon.

#25 MAKE YOUR OWN SMOOTHIES

Budget: $$$ Time: 🕐🕐🕐🕐🕐

Smoothies are a delicious way to increase your intake of fresh fruit and vegetables. Home-made smoothies are fresher and tastier (not to mention cheaper) than anything you can buy in the shops. And drunk in moderation they are really good for you too.

To make your own smoothies, the only tool you will need is a blender or food processor. You can make smoothies with fruit and/or vegetables. Veggie smoothies can be healthier because they have less sugar, but fruit smoothies are, of course, a lot more popular!

Most people use fresh fruit to make smoothies, but frozen fruit also works well, and even canned or dried. You can limit yourself to one fruit, or add two or more – experimenting with different combinations to find ones you like is part of the fun! The following can all make delicious smoothies: peaches, strawberries, blueberries, raspberries, blackcurrants, bananas, apples, kiwis, mangoes, avocados, pears and pomegranates.

Fruits with high water content such as oranges, pineapples and watermelons can also work well in smoothies. Just bear in mind that they will make your smoothie more watery, and adjust the recipe accordingly. Some popular starter combinations include raspberry and apple, mango and peach, and strawberry and banana.

As well as fruit, you will need to add some liquid. Milk is a popular choice, and you can use whole or skimmed. Soy milk is good for people who are lactose intolerant, and adds protein as well. Other possibilities include yogurt, ice cream, and sparkling water (try lime or lemon flavors). If you have nothing else, ordinary water will be fine too. One to two cups of liquid should be sufficient.

Once all the ingredients are in the blender, add a few ice cubes. Start the machine on a low to medium setting, and turn it up as the fruit and ice cubes break down. Once your concoction looks fairly smooth – which shouldn't take longer than a minute ¬– turn off the blender and let the drink settle. Pour it into a chilled glass, garnish with a slice of fresh fruit or a sprig of mint, and enjoy!

More Tips

• To make your smoothies healthier you can add vegetables as well. Kale and spinach blend in well, and you probably won't even be able to taste them. Celery and beetroot are good healthy options too.

• Don't over-blend your smoothies, or they will become like milk shakes.

• If you're worried your smoothie won't be sweet enough, add ripe bananas, maple syrup or honey. You can also add plain sugar, but this won't be as healthy.

• There are other ingredients you can experiment with as well. Try coconut shavings (great with pineapple), vanilla extract, cinnamon, cayenne pepper, peanut butter or Nutella. Adding these can give your smoothies a whole new dimension. Just don't overdo it!

#26 ORGANIZE A TREASURE HUNT

Budget: $$$ Time: ⏱⏱⏱⏱⏱

Treasure hunts are fun for both children and adults. They are also enjoyable (if challenging) to plan and organize as well!

Treasure hunts take participants from one location to another via a series of clues, until they reach the final destination where the 'treasure' is to be found. The first to get there claims the prize, although there may also be consolation prizes for later arrivals. Treasure hunts can be played by individuals, but are often more fun (and work better) when the players are in pairs or teams.

One good thing about treasure hunts is that they are suitable for all ages, from young children to adults. Obviously, clues should be easier for children, and the locations within a smaller area (your home and garden, for example). With adults you can set more challenging clues, and if you wish use a much wider area as well.

The key to a successful treasure hunt is coming up with good clues that will make contestants think but not baffle them. For young children, a clue such as 'Where tomatoes are grown' directing them to the greenhouse might be a good choice. For adults, clues can be more challenging. Riddles, rhymes, puns, close-up photos of the next destination and anagrams can all be good choices.

More Tips

• When planning a hunt, work backwards from the final location.

• Make the first clues easy and later ones harder (but not impossible).

• Be sure to zigzag and cross paths several times to keep the hunters guessing about the final destination.

• Try to find creative places to hide clues, such as taped under chairs or inside garbage lids.

• Don't make clues too difficult to reach. Put them in places that will be easily spotted by the hunters, but (if outside your home) won't be noticed by too many casual passers-by.

• Make the playing area large enough so that everyone won't be moving round in a group together. A large house and garden would be fine, or perhaps a park or other open space. For adults you could use the whole town, but don't make it too wide an area to limit the time taken and any travel costs. Obviously, explain to players at the start the area within which they should search.

• Treasure hunts often work best if themed. With children you could have a theme of pirates looking for buried treasure or a futuristic space voyage. With adults, the theme could be a popular movie, musical or TV show.

As organizer, you will obviously be excluded from taking part in the hunt, but there is still plenty you can do. You could get involved at each location, providing encouragement and refreshments. You could also challenge players to a game or puzzle before revealing the next clue.

Whatever you do, though, don't tell anyone the answers, or the others will feel it is unfair. Most of all, make sure everyone has fun and stays safe throughout the entire hunt.

#27 PLAY A ♠♣♥♦
CARD GAME

Budget: $$$ Time: 🕐🕐🕐🕐🕐

Almost every home has a deck of cards lying around somewhere, and there are hundreds, probably thousands, of games you can play with them.

If there's just you, you could play patience (there are many different versions to choose from). But obviously it's more fun if there are two or more of you. Here are three card games that are easy to learn and can provide hours of fun for all the family.

1. Cheat
Deal all the cards. The first player places one card face down and calls 'Ace'. The next puts another card on this, calling 'Two'. The next lays a card and calls 'Three'. And so on, all the way through Jack, Queen, King, and back to Ace, Two, Three again.

Of course, nobody can see the card you're putting down. So you can cheat by disposing of any card in your hand, regardless of the number you call. But you must pretend to keep the sequence going.

If anyone suspects you of cheating, they can call out 'Cheat!' Your card must then be turned over. If it shows you've cheated, you must pick up the whole pile. If you were telling the truth, the challenger must pick up the pile. The winner is the first to dispose of all their cards.

2. Black Maria
This game works best with 3 to 5 players. The aim is to avoid winning any tricks with Hearts in them, and especially to avoid winning with the Queen of Spades. Each Heart counts as 1 point against its winner, and the Queen of Spades counts for 13.

The player to the dealer's left leads first. After that, whoever wins the trick leads next. A player may lead with anything they like. The other players must follow suit if possible. If they can't, they can play any card. The trick is won by the highest card of the suit led.

At the end of the hand, players count up their winning tricks, receiving 1 penalty point for each Heart, and 13 for the Queen of Spades. Play continues till one player reaches 50 points. The player with the lowest total is then declared the winner.

3. Pig

This is a great party game. Use a pack with 4 cards of the same rank for each player and discard the rest, for example with four players you could just use the aces, kings, queens and jacks (16 cards). Deal so every player has 4 cards.

When the dealer says 'Go!' pick one card you don't wish to keep, along with everyone else, and put it face down on your left. You're trying to get 4 matching cards, so only put down one that doesn't match anything you have.

Pick up the card from the player on your right. Choose another card to pass when the dealer says 'Go!' again, and continue till someone holds 4 matching cards. Anyone doing this must put a finger on the tip of their nose. On seeing this, everyone else must do likewise. The last to do so earns a 'P', and is eliminated when he has earned all three letters P-I-G. The last one left is the winner!

#28 LEARN A MAGIC TRICK

Budget: $$$ Time: 🕐🕐🕒🕒🕐

Impress your friends and family – and maybe even start a new career! – by learning one or two simple magic tricks.

Everyone is fascinated by magic (or conjuring if you prefer) and anyone can learn to perform some basic tricks with just a little practice and preparation.

Here are two easy tricks to get you started:

Make a Coin Disappear

In this trick it looks to the audience as if you are moving a coin from your left hand to your right, and then making it disappear in your right hand.

In reality, you keep the coin in your left hand the whole time, while tricking your audience into thinking you moved it. This is how you do it…

• Hold the coin between the thumb and first two fingers of your left hand.

• Move your right hand towards the left, pretending to reach down to pick it up with your three middle fingers, while in reality letting it drop into the palm of your left hand.

• Pretend you're holding it between the index finger and thumb of your right hand.

• Blow on your right hand and open it, showing that the coin has disappeared.

• Reach with your left hand towards your elbow and reveal the coin, making it look like that was where you made it vanish to.

Make a Card Disappear

For this trick, you place a card in your hand and snap your fingers. To the audience it looks as though the card disappears. This is how you do it…

• Hold your hand with the index and pinkie fingers up and the other three fingers touching each other.
• Place the card with the last inch tucked into the area between the middle and ring finger and thumb.
• Gently snap your fingers and straighten out your hand. The card will be clipped between your first and second finger and third and fourth finger, and will seem to have vanished. Just ensure you're facing the audience with your palm so they can't see the card on the other side of your hand.
• As you get more skillful, you can practice bringing the card back and making it disappear again.

<u>More Magic Tips</u>

• Practice in front of a mirror so you can see the trick as your audience will. The more you practice, the smoother your act will become.

• Know in advance what you're going to say. Good patter will distract the audience just enough to keep them from working out how you pulled off your trick!

• Resist the temptation to give away how a trick was done. Keep the audience guessing and they will be more impressed with your skills.

• Whenever possible, borrow objects such as coins and pens from the audience. This will make the tricks seem more impressive, as you won't have had time to do anything sneaky to the item concerned.

• If you get the bug for magic, there are many more amazing tricks you can learn. The internet has some great free resources, including www. goodtricks.net and http://easybartricks.com. Try also searching YouTube. com for videos of magic tricks.

#29 TAKE UP DANCING

Budget: $$$ Time: 🕐🕐🕐🕐🕐

Dancing is a great way of getting fit while having fun. And it can be a very sociable activity as well.

Anyone can learn to dance, whatever their age or background. And nowadays it's just as socially acceptable for men to dance as for women.

The first step is to choose a dance style that appeals to you. There are lots of possibilities, including ballet, disco, tap, jazz, ballroom, swing, hip-hop, Latin American, break-dancing, modern, Irish, and even belly dancing. You'll find hundreds of how-to videos online for all styles to help you choose. And, of course, you should take any opportunity you can to see live performances as well.

When you've chosen a style, start by trying the moves at home, following advice from a book or DVD or on the internet. See how it feels, and how you look performing the moves in a full-length mirror.

If you want to go further, the next step will be to enroll in a class. Classes are available in most dance forms, and it's often possible to book a trial lesson free or inexpensively to see if it's something you enjoy.

Continue to practice at home and attend classes, and you'll soon see your skill level improve, and your fitness along with it. Surely that's better than yet another night at home watching TV!

More Tips

• If you haven't done any physical exercise for a while, don't overdo it or you could injure yourself. If you're seriously out of shape, it may be a good idea to do some general fitness training before you start a dance class.

• Wearing the appropriate clothes and shoes will make you feel more comfortable and help protect you from injuries. Ask in advance for advice, but don't over-invest in expensive outfits or shoes if you're still not sure this is for you.

• Begin any dance session with a warm-up, including stretching to improve your flexibility and reduce the chances of injury.

• If possible, go to classes with a friend (or your other half). As well as a ready-made dance partner, this will give you someone to support and encourage you if your motivation flags.

• Aim to follow a healthy, balanced diet, and keep yourself hydrated. The latter is especially important for the more energetic types of dance.

• When you are improving, sign up for a dancing competition. This will give you a target to aim for, and win or lose it will give you a sense of achievement.

• Never just dance the steps. Get into the music, and put some feeling into it. If it's an upbeat, happy dance, make strong, sharp movements, and smile! If it's a sad or emotional dance, use this to guide your expression and moves. Dance is a performance art, and dancing with emotion will make it more enjoyable for you and for people watching you as well.

#30 VISIT A MUSEUM OR ART GALLERY

Budget: $$$ Time: 🕐🕑🕒🕓🕔

For an inspiring and thought-provoking change of scene, why not pay a visit to a local museum or gallery?

Some are free, while most are inexpensive, and many offer group or family discounts as well. Most museums and galleries nowadays make every effort to make their exhibits exciting and engaging. The old image of these places as lifeless and boring is a thing of the past now!

Your first step in planning a visit will be to decide what type of museum or gallery most appeals to you. There are lots of options here, although obviously the range of choice will depend on where you live. Some possibilities include:

- History museums
- Science museums
- Transportation museums
- Art (and sculpture) galleries
- Living museums (with live actors/performers)
- Natural history museums
- Specialty museums

Specialty museums cover a huge range of topics, some quite surprising. Examples include the Museum of Wooden Nickels in San Antonio, the Asphalt Museum in Rohnert Park, California, and the Cumberland Pencil Museum, in Cumbria, England.

Museums nowadays offer a lot more than just exhibits in glass cases. Increasingly, they are becoming important centers in the local community as well – places where people come to talk to friends and neighbors, plan projects, and share their culture and experiences. Many host talks by experts, book signings, and classes for adults and children. Some even run concerts, wine festivals and farmers' markets!

To make the most of your visit, it's important to prepare beforehand.

Nowadays most places have a website, and often a Facebook page as well. Use this to check opening hours and days (some smaller museums only open on certain days of the week, or just in the mornings or afternoons). Find out what they charge for entry, and if there are any discounts you are eligible for.

It's also a good idea to research any exhibits you particularly want to see, and whether there are any special events, displays or exhibitions you can take in while you are there.

Finally, check if there is somewhere you can get refreshments. A day wandering around a museum can make you both hungry and thirsty!

More Tips

• Take a friend (or friends). Visiting museums is always more fun when you're with someone else to share the experience and talk about what you're seeing.

• Many museums and galleries offer tours. Check in advance or when you arrive, and see if there are any you could join. A tour led by an expert guide will give you a whole new perspective on the exhibits, and you can ask questions as well.

#31 CREATE A WILDLIFE GARDEN

Budget: $$$ Time: ◷◷◷◷◷

All over the world, wildlife is struggling to survive, largely due to the disruption to habitats caused by human beings.

By making your garden more wildlife-friendly, you can help restore the natural balance. Whether you have an apartment balcony or a forty-acre farm, you can create a garden that attracts beautiful wildlife and helps it thrive.

Creating a wildlife garden involves more than just letting part of your garden grow wild (though that can certainly help). Here are a number of other things you can do to make your patch more hospitable to small animals, birds and insects:

Build a Pond

A pool of water – even a puddle a few inches deep in an upturned trashcan lid – will attract plenty of wildlife into your garden, from dragonflies and bats to frogs and newts. But don't add goldfish – they eat smaller animals and encourage algal blooms.

Provide Food

Every creature has to eat. Planting native plants or hanging feeders in safe places are two easy ways to make your garden into a gourmet restaurant for wildlife! Native flowers, shrubs and trees provide the foliage, nectar, berries, seeds and nuts that many species of wildlife need to live and thrive.

Choose Pollinator-Friendly Plants

Many plants bred in recent years have done pollinating insects such as bees no favors. The fashion for elaborate double-flowers that don't allow access to pollen or nectar has led to a drastic decline in their numbers.

But nowadays a resurgence in more traditional plants is well under way. Aim to buy plants that are labeled pollinator-friendly. This means you can provide a long and uninterrupted season of such flowers, from crocuses, single-flowered snowdrops and hellebores in the winter, through to asters and anemones in the fall.

Give Birds Somewhere to Live

It's easy to buy (or build) nest boxes suitable for almost every garden bird imaginable, from owls to finches, robins to sparrows. Position boxes in safe, secure places where they will not be vulnerable to marauding cats or other predators. Be patient, as it may be a while before you get any residents.

Give Insects a Home Too

They may not be as photogenic as birds, but without insects, most plants (including fruit trees) wouldn't be pollinated and birds would go hungry. Insect hotels have become a popular purchase in recent years, but many are too small to have much impact. If you have the space, think about creating a wildlife stack instead, using old wooden pallets, roof tiles, plant pots, bricks, stones and so on. You can make a surprisingly attractive garden feature this way.

By following these simple tips, you can create a beautiful garden that attracts a wide range of wildlife, and provides far more interest and variety than most of what is on TV!

#32 BECOME A TV SHOW CONTESTANT

Budget: $$$ Time: ◔◔◔◔◔

Rather than sitting at home watching TV, why not become a part of it yourself as a TV show contestant?

There are many opportunities for people to appear in TV shows. In recent years 'reality television' featuring ordinary people in a range of scenarios, from dating to surviving in inhospitable places, has become extremely popular.

Talent shows are also massive across the world right now. If you can sing, dance, perform acrobatics, or have some other talent people might like to watch, there's almost certainly a show you can apply for.

Another popular option is quiz/game shows, from *Who Wants to be a Millionaire* to *The Price is Right*. A steady stream of contestants is needed for these as well.

Aside from the possibility of fame or fortune, being in a TV show can be an exciting and eye-opening experience. You will see what goes on behind the scenes at your favorite shows, and will watch them with fresh appreciation in future. And, of course, you will have an experience to remember and tell your friends about for months and years to come!

Applying and Auditioning

You can find out what shows are currently recruiting by contacting the production companies directly. See who makes a show that you would like to appear on and look them up online.

There are also websites that publish contestant calls. In the US, RealityWanted.com lists lots of opportunities for reality shows, game shows and quiz shows. In the UK, BeOnScreen.com is a good place to start.

To be accepted as a contestant, you will normally need to go through some sort of audition process. Big TV talent shows such as *American Idol* and *X Factor* typically hold open auditions in major cities across the country.

To get on a quiz or reality show you will probably have to perform an initial test/audition as well, though it will be lower key. These auditions are generally held by specialist companies who recruit contestants for the shows. They will assess your personality and appearance, and how well you are able to communicate. They may also check your ability to cope under stress (so don't get flustered if an alarm goes off mid-audition – this can be part of the testing process).

If you're auditioning for a quiz show you may be given a series of questions to answer, to test your general knowledge. If you find them all easy it may nevertheless be a good strategy to deliberately get one or two wrong: nobody likes a smartass!

If you're selected, arrive in good time at the studio and introduce yourself to the researchers. They are likely to ask a few questions about your family, job, hobbies, and so on. This is to give the host or hostess something to talk about.

Once the show starts, try to relax and concentrate on the task in hand. Do your best to succeed, but remember that not everyone can win. Smile and be courteous to the host and (especially) your fellow contestants. This will ensure the audience like you and get behind you, which can help a lot when you're under pressure.

Good luck, and we hope you win a million!

#33 TRY YOUR HAND AT BONSAI

Budget: $$$ Time: 🕐🕐🕐🕐🕐

Bonsai is the ancient Japanese art of growing full-size trees in miniature. It takes time and is not an activity for anyone needing instant gratification, but for those with patience it can be a surprisingly satisfying and absorbing hobby.

The bonsai effect is achieved through careful cultivation and judicious pruning. It does not require special plants or growth-restricting hormones.

It is possible to bonsai almost any tree, though some are more suitable than others. Here are some species that are generally regarded as most suitable for beginners:

• Juniper
• Ficus (Fig)
• Chinese Elm
• Jade
• Dwarf Schefflera (Arboricola)

Note that some plants such as Juniper do best when grown outside, while others such as the Chinese Elm are suitable for indoor cultivation.

When deciding where to start, aim to choose a tree that grows well in gardens in your area and is easily obtainable. Look for a healthy plant, not one that is deformed or distorted. Don't sacrifice health and structure for a few extra years of age. Start with a tree that is small enough for you to manage easily.

When potting a bonsai tree, it's important to use the right kind of soil. A bonsai container or pot is an unnatural and restrictive environment for a tree, and it therefore requires very well-drained soil with a mixture of organic and inorganic compounds. Bonsai soils that work well in one place may not work as well in your own back yard. If possible, therefore, ask for advice from a local bonsai supplier or an enthusiast who has experience growing bonsai in your area.

<u>More Tips</u>

• Watering is one of the most crucial things to get right. Bonsai need to be watered regularly but not over-watered.

• They also need regular fertilizer, which should only be applied after they have been watered.

• To grow your bonsai to the desired shape while keeping it small, you will need to prune it regularly. A pair of specialist bonsai shears is ideal for this.

• Bonsai need to be repotted from time to time, to prune the roots and refresh the soil. Repotting is best done in the early spring, and not in the middle of the growing season.

• Many areas have clubs for bonsai lovers, and these can be great for getting tips and advice from experienced growers.

There are numerous books you can buy to learn more about bonsai – garden centers usually have a selection, or you could search the Amazon online bookstore. There are also some excellent websites aimed at beginners, including BonsaiExperience.com and BonsaiforBeginners.com.

#34 LEARN TO TIE KNOTS

Budget: $$$ Time: 🕐🕐🕐🕐🕐

Okay, so everyone knows how to tie a basic 'granny' knot. But there are dozens of other knots you can learn as well, all with their own special uses. Some are mainly used on ships, but others can be invaluable in many other circumstances as well.

And it's not just for showing off to your friends either. The right knot can save lives when you're in a survival situation, performing first aid, or working over heights or on water.

Here are five basic knots everyone should know:

1. Square Knot
Also known as a reef knot, this is a simple, quick knot for tying two ropes together. It's popular among sailors, climbers and outdoorsmen for its speed. You tie it by lapping right over left, and then tying again in the reverse direction, left over right.

2. Figure of Eight
This knot is used for creating a stopper at the end of a rope or line. It's also known as a Flemish Knot. To make it you pass the free end of the line over itself to form a loop. Continue under and around the line's end, and finish by passing the free end down through the loop.

3. Clove Hitch
The Clove Hitch is another easy knot and can be used to secure a line to a tree or post quickly. It can slip when used alone, so should not be used in high-strain situations without another knot or knots as backup. To create a Clove Hitch on a tree, loop the rope around it. Then make another loop and pass the free end of the rope under the second loop before tightening it.

4. Bowline

This knot is used to create a loop at the end of a rope that can't shrink or grow. It is often taught with the story of a rabbit coming out of his hole, in front of a tree, going behind the tree, and back down his original hole. In basic terms, you form a loop on top of the long end of the line. Pass the free end of the line through the loop and around behind the line. Bring the free end down in the original loop, while maintaining the secondary loop, which becomes your Bowline loop. Once the 'rabbit' is back down his hole, pull the 'tree' up and the Bowline is tightened.

5. Sheet Bend

This knot is used for tying different types of material together and joining different thicknesses of rope. To tie it, you bend the thicker or more slippery rope into a 'J' shape (like a fish-hook). You then pass the other rope through the fish hook from behind, wrap around the entire hook once, and then tuck the smaller line under itself.

One other very important tip is that once you have made any knot, be sure to pull it tight to stop it slipping.

• There are some excellent interactive websites where you can watch knots such as those above and many others being tied. This can be invaluable for mastering the steps required. Netknots.com and AnimatedKnots.com are two great free resources to start with.

#35 START A DIARY

Budget: $$$ Time: ◷◷◷◷◷

In recent times keeping a diary has rather fallen out of fashion. In the past, though, among the educated classes at any rate, it was extremely popular.

Some diaries such as those of Samuel Pepys in 17th century London and Anne Frank in Nazi-occupied Amsterdam have become important historical documents, providing fascinating glimpses into everyday life at the time.

Even if you aren't concerned about going down in history, however, keeping a diary can be an absorbing pastime and a great aid to self-analysis and problem-solving. And you will have an ever-growing record of your thoughts and activities to look back over. This can be helpful for measuring your progress in life, reminding yourself of happy times, and even sharing memories with younger generations in future.

It's best to set a particular time of day for updating your diary. Many people like to do it last thing at night, which is obviously a good time to reflect on what has happened that day. Morning or night, having a set time will help you get into a regular routine for completing your diary.

More Tips

• Regard your diary as a close friend. You will be entrusting your deepest secrets to it, after all!

• Keep it in a secure place that is safe from prying eyes. If possible, get one that is lockable.

• Write neatly. You want to be able to read your diary in a few years' time without struggling to decipher what you meant!

• If for some reason you don't have a chance to write in your diary for a while, don't stress, but update it with everything that has happened when you get the chance.

• You don't have to stick to just writing. If you are artistic, you could include drawings and sketches as well, or stickers and doodles. You could also print out photos and include them.

• If you prefer to complete your diary on a computer, that's fine as well. By adding a password you can pretty much guarantee its security (as long as it's not too easy to guess).

• Try not to write in your diary more than once a day. If something drastic happens that you must write about, put 'Later' under the part you already wrote.

• If keeping an ordinary diary doesn't appeal, how about a nature diary? This works best if you have a garden, of course, or perhaps there is a park or other open area you visit regularly. Record the plants, birds, insects and animals you see, and any other interesting observations about them. Over time this can provide a valuable record of changes to the natural environment.

#36 GIVE YOUR CAR A VALET SERVICE

Budget: $$$ Time: 🕐🕐🕐🕐🕐

Be honest – when did you last show your car a bit of TLC? If you're like most of us you take it for granted as long as it gets you from A to B, and let the dirt and dust build up inside and out.

The good news is that it's easy, quick and cheap to give your car a thorough 'valet service' and get it back in (almost) showroom condition.

It's best to choose a warm, sunny day for doing this, so the car will dry out quickly afterwards. Then just follow the steps below:

1. Wash the exterior with a car shampoo and sponge, then rinse and polish with a chamois leather. Don't forget to clean the headlamps and wing mirrors as well.

2. Clear out all the garbage that has accumulated, including candy wrappers, drink cartons, pay-and-display car park tickets, and so on.

3. Using a vacuum cleaner hose or portable car vacuum, clear out any dirt, crumbs, grit and plant matter on the seats and on the floor. You can also use a dry brush for this.

4. Clean the dashboard and any other plastic areas with a soft, damp cloth. Once you've done that, go over it again with car wax or protectant.

5. If your car has any leather in its interior, use a proprietary leather cleaner on this and follow the instructions carefully. Be careful to avoid rubbing too hard, as this can damage the leather.

How to Clean Fabric Car Seats

Fabric seats can be big collectors of dirt, dust and other assorted gunk.

Fortunately it's easy to clean them and leave them smelling fresh and new. All you need is a few inexpensive household items:

2 tablespoons dish soap
2 tablespoons washing soda
2 cups hot water
Mixing bowl or bucket
Cleaning brush
Towel (clean and dry)
Linen spray (optional)

Once you have assembled these items, follow the steps below:

1. Remove any loose dirt with a dry brush or vacuum cleaner, as described above.

2. Mix the dish soap, washing soda and hot water to create a cleaning solution. The dish soap will gently lift any stains while refreshing the fabric, and washing soda is a cleaning booster. Both are safe to use on fabrics. Give the solution a quick whisk.

3. Dip the cleaning brush in the liquid and work it over the car seats in a circular motion. Avoid soaking the fabric – you simply want to dampen it to lift any stains. This process also helps remove any pilling from the upholstery.

4. Dry the seat by dabbing it repeatedly with the towel, and continue until all the seats have been cleaned. Lower the windows and allow the seats to dry out completely.

5. Finish by giving the seats another vacuum, and spritz them with linen spray. You'll love your fragrant-smelling vehicle!

This whole process shouldn't take more than an hour, and you'll appreciate the benefits every time you get into your car in future. Your passengers will thank you for it too!

#37 CREATE A LITTLE FREE LIBRARY

Budget: $$$ Time: 🕐🕐🕐🕐🕐

If you enjoy reading books, why not share the love by creating a Little Free Library?

The first Little Free Library was created in 2009 by a Wisconsin man named Todd Boll. He created a small wooden house just large enough for twenty books and put it on a post at the end of his drive with a sign saying 'Free Books'. Before long his idea became a book-sharing movement across the whole of the US, and now the world.

The idea of Little Free Libraries is that they are 'take a book, return a book' gathering places, where neighbors can share their favorite literature and stories. In its most basic form, a Little Free Library is a box full of books where anyone may stop by and pick up a book (or two) and bring back others to share.

Making Your Own Little Free Library

Creating your own library is easy. All you really need is a box with at least one shelf fixed to a post that won't tip over (cement it to the ground if you can). There are building plans on the Little Free Libraries website at LittleFreeLibrary.org, or you could simply adapt a bird table or rabbit hutch for this purpose.

Books don't like damp, so one important thing you will need to do is weatherproof your box. Give it several coats of paint or varnish, and line every surface with waterproofing membrane, available in DIY stores.

Positioning

Put your library in a place that can be easily seen from your home but isn't too close to your front door – at the end of the drive, beside the gate or above a decorative shrub in the garden, perhaps. Making it easily visible will encourage more users, and also deter possible vandalism.

Some people may not understand the free library concept or think there is a catch, so make a sign explaining that anyone is welcome to take a book and/or leave a book, and the more people who do so, the more books will pass through.

More Tips

• Create a small guest book in the library, attached by a chain, in which people can leave comments or reviews.
• Register your library at LittleFreeLibrary.org. You'll then get a dot on their world-wide map and an official sign.
• But don't forget to spread the word locally as well. Tell your neighbors, family and friends, and put it on Facebook, Instagram, Twitter, and so on. Inform your local church and school as well.

Finally, encourage other people to follow your lead, and soon you could have a whole mini-community of Little Free Libraries in your neighborhood!

#38 TAKE UP PAINTING

Budget: $$$ **Time: 🕐🕐🕐🕐🕐**

You may have heard it takes talent to paint, but that's really a myth. OK, you might never be another Van Gogh, but anyone can learn to paint to a reasonable standard. All it takes is enthusiasm and a willingness to learn.

Having decided to paint, your first decision will be what method you're going to use. There are four main choices, each with its own advantages and disadvantages.

Watercolor

This is the sort of painting we all did as children. Its advantages include being very cheap, you can do it anywhere, and it's easy to clean your brushes (and yourself) afterward. Because watercolor is quite transparent, it can be hard to cover up any mistakes. You also have to allow for the fact that colors typically became lighter once they've dried.

Acrylic

Acrylic paints have the advantage that they dry very fast, and once a layer has dried it's easy to paint over. They are also water-soluble. They are more expensive than watercolors, and they dry hard, so you will need to wash your brushes as soon as possible after using them.

Oil Paint

The main choice of the Old Masters, oil paint has many advantages for serious artists. The colors are rich and deep and don't change as the paint dries. Oils can also be over-painted once dry without disturbing the underlying layers. You will need to work in a well-ventilated area and clean your brushes with a solvent. Paintings can take weeks or even months to dry, so many artists work on several at once.

Pastels

Pastels can give a 'painted' effect while retaining the immediacy of drawing. There is no waiting for them to dry, and colors are mixed on paper rather than a palette by overlaying or blending them. On the minus side, colors can be tricky to blend, and soft pastel in particular is liable to smudging.

There is no right or wrong method, and the best advice is to try a number and see which you feel most comfortable with. Acrylics are a popular choice for beginners and can be used on just about any surface, including paper, canvas or board. But if you prefer watercolor or pastels, or even oils, there's no reason you couldn't start there.

<u>More Tips</u>

• Buy the best quality paint you can afford, but not so expensive that you're worried to waste some.

• Learn the basics of color theory, and especially color mixing

• Consider enrolling in a class to improve your technique. There may also be a local amateur artists' group you could join.

• Have fun, and give yourself the freedom to experiment. Once you have a few paintings you are proud of, consider entering them in a contest or offering them for an exhibition.

• There is lots of advice online for aspiring painters – try http://painting. about.com and paintdrawpaint.com for starters. You can also search on YouTube for videos featuring practical demonstrations of painting techniques.

#39 THROW A PARTY

Budget: $$$ Time: ◷◷◷◷◷

Everyone loves a party. If the invitations have been a bit thin on the ground recently, why not organize one of your own?

You don't have to look far to find a reason for a party. As well as birthdays, they might include starting a new job, moving home, an anniversary, an academic achievement, a sporting success or an engagement. Or you could simply throw a party to celebrate the season, a festival or holiday, or simply being alive!

One thing that can help any party go with a swing is if you have a theme. For example, if there is a major international sporting event coming up – the Olympic Games, say – you could base your party around that. Ask guests to wear the relevant national colors, decorate the house accordingly, and provide suitably themed food and drink. You could also plan some Olympics-related party games.

Be sure to have a good selection of food, especially if some guests will be coming a long way. Finger foods that people can easily pick up and eat work best, such as pizza slices, quiche, sandwiches, potato chips and sausage rolls. Don't forget to cater for vegetarians and any friends on special diets too. But avoid planning dishes that will require cooking during the party itself – you want to be mingling with your guests and enjoying their company, not trapped in the kitchen all night.

More Tips

• Give people plenty of notice. This will reduce the chances they already have something arranged.

• Invite more people than you plan on having, as inevitably some won't turn up.

• Ask people to let you know if they will be attending. This can't be relied on, but will give you some idea of likely numbers.

• Only invite people you really want at your party. Avoid inviting anyone you think would be negative and spoil the atmosphere for everyone else.

• Avoid issuing open invitations. It's normal to let guests bring a friend or partner, but not to invite lots of people you don't know.

• Make sure you have suitable music lined up – plan to play quieter tracks early on while people are talking and eating, and livelier stuff later when they are in the mood to dance.

• Always have a spare room ready in your house in case someone needs to stay over.

• As host/hostess, be sure to talk to everybody (especially the quieter ones) and ask how they are doing. Take the opportunity to introduce friends who may not know each other, and point out anything they have in common.

• Put plenty of garbage cans and bags out in all of the rooms. The easier it is for guests to throw away their trash, the more likely they are to do it, which means less cleaning up for you.

Above all, relax, and have a great time!

#40 MAKE YOUR OWN
PODCAST

Budget: $$$ Time: 🕐🕐🕐🕐🕐

If you've ever listened to a radio talk show and thought you could do better, why not put it to the test by creating your very own podcast?

Podcasting is essentially blogging for the spoken word. A podcast is an audio file, usually in MP3 format. They are called podcasts because they can be listened to on an Apple iPod. But they can also, of course, be played on any MP3 player or on a computer. Many people nowadays listen to podcasts on their smartphones.

According to the latest statistics, over a third of all Americans have listened to a podcast, and the trend is being repeated in many other parts of the world too. Podcasts focus on all kinds of subjects, from science to comedy, politics to film and media. Often they take a witty and irreverent approach to the topic in question.

Popular podcasts include Mugglecast, which covers 'Harry Potter' novels and films; The Word Nerds, which discusses the origins of words and other linguistic matters; and Tech Weekly, the Guardian newspaper tech team's podcast, with news and discussion from the digital worlds of technology, gaming and the internet.

Creating your own podcasts is actually quite simple. There are really only three things you need:

1. a good-quality microphone
2. an audio recording program
3. access to the internet

For their recording program, many podcasters use the free Audacity software. You can download this from http://audacity.sourceforge.net. There are also in-depth tutorials and help files available via the Audacity website, not to mention a thriving user community.

Once your podcast has been recorded and edited, you will need to upload it to some podcast sites so that people can listen to it. Here are a few possibilities:

• PodOMatic.com
• PodcastAlley.com
• iTunes.com
• PodcastDirectory.com
• PodNova.com

If you have a website or blog it's a good idea to make your podcast available from there too. Alternatively – or as well – you could set up a free page on the PodOmatic website and host your podcast there. This has the advantage that you will get access to detailed statistics on who is downloading your podcasts, and you will become a member of their world-wide podcasting community.

Podcasting can be great fun, and many people find it quite addictive. You will hear from people across the world who have listened to your podcast and want to discuss it with you. In addition, if your podcast builds up a large following, you may be able to make money from it, e.g. by selling advertising. Note, however, that while a very few podcasts are able to charge their subscribers, the great majority are distributed free.

#41 GO BIRD-WATCHING

Budget: $$$ Time: 🕐🕐🕐🕐🕐

Bird-watching, or birding as it's also known, is an increasingly popular hobby in many parts of the world.

Going out to look for (and listen to) different species of birds in your locality can be both enriching and relaxing. It also has the attraction of being free of charge, you get some fresh air and exercise, and it's suitable for all the family.

You don't need to go anywhere special to start bird-watching. If you have a garden you will see a variety of birds there, but if not all you need do is take a stroll to your local park. As you become more enthusiastic you may want to visit other wilder places, such as forests, woodland, meadows, mudflats, ponds and lakes. At the latter you will be able to observe large water birds such as ducks, geese, or herons.

Although you can bird-watch with the naked eye, a good pair of binoculars will let you see the birds much more clearly. This will enhance your enjoyment, as well as making them easier to identify. A light-weight pair with reasonable magnification (e.g. 7x or 8x) often works best in cluttered environments such as forest or woodland. Higher magnification (10x or 12x) glasses are better for open country and wetland birding.

The other thing you will want in order to get the most from this activity is a good field guide. This should include full-color illustrations of the types of bird you are likely to see in your locale, together with advice on identifying them and any other interesting features.

More Tips

• Choose a time of day when birds are most plentiful – early morning or late afternoon is often best.

• Dress in comfortable clothes that will be appropriate for the weather (check the forecast beforehand). If you'll be out for a while take snacks and drinks. If it's a bright sunny day, remember to put on sunscreen.

• At home, set out bird feeders with nuts, seeds, and so on – this is a great way to attract a variety of species. But ensure you don't position it where birds will be vulnerable to cats or other predators.

• You can also install a bird bath or fountain. Running or dripping water especially interests birds.

• Don't get too close to birds, especially if they are nesting. This will stress them, and could cause them to abandon their young.

• Keep a notebook and record your observations in this. Many bird-watchers enjoy keeping a list of birds they have seen, especially when they are able to add a new and rare species!

Finally, if you find you really enjoy bird-watching, search online for birding groups near you. Many such groups lead bird walks you can attend. You could also contact local universities or parks to find out whether any classes or walks are organized. The more of you there are on a walk, the more birds you're likely to observe, especially if you go with bird-watchers who are more experienced than you.

#42 TAKE UP CLOUDSPOTTING

Budget: $$$ Time: 🕐🕐🕐🕐🕐

Cloudspotting is a great antidote to the pressures and stresses of life in the 21st century. It must count as one of the most restful hobbies ever invented, and can also help you learn about and predict the weather. You need never be surprised by a sudden shower or storm again!

Anyone who can see the sky can do this wherever they are in the world. And there is no need to spend any money, though for added enjoyment you might want to take binoculars and a camera, and perhaps a notebook to record your observations.

Clouds are made up of water droplets or – in colder temperatures – ice crystals. They form due to the Earth's atmosphere becoming saturated due to one or both of two processes: cooling of the air and the addition of water vapor. When the air becomes sufficiently saturated, rain (or in colder temperatures snow or hail) will fall to the surface.

The taller clouds are, the less light they let through, so the darker they appear (and the more likely they are to result in rain).

Clouds can take all manner of shapes and sizes. Part of the fun of cloudspotting is looking out for clouds that resemble something else: a human face, perhaps, a pointing hand, or maybe even a tiger waiting to pounce!

The classic book on cloudspotting is The Cloudspotters Guide by British author Gavin Pretor-Pinney, founder of the Cloud Appreciation Society. This ever-so-slightly tongue-in-cheek book explains about all the main types of cloud and how and why they form. The author shares lots of fascinating facts about clouds in his book, combining humor with hard science.

Clouds can be roughly divided into three broad categories according to where in the atmosphere they form:

High Clouds	**Middle Clouds**	**Low-to-Middle Clouds**
Cirrus	Altocumulus	Cumulus
Cirrocumulus	Altostratus	Stratus
Cirrostratus		Nimbostratus
		Cumulonimbus

Cirrus clouds are wispy and white, and sometimes likened to mares' tails. Like 'cotton wool' cumulus clouds, which form lower down in the atmosphere, they are generally associated with fine weather.

By contrast, darker nimbostratus clouds generally portend rain. And if you see towering cumulonimbus clouds, you had better seek shelter quickly from the coming storm!

For more information (and pictures) the Cloud Appreciation Society, mentioned above, has a website at http://cloudappreciationsociety.org. This has literally thousands of photos submitted by members, many of them stunningly beautiful. You can also search the site for clouds that look like something else, or for particular types of cloud if you need help identifying them.

#43 WRITE A POEM

Budget: $$$ **Time:** 🕐🕐🕐🕐🕐

For hundreds of years people have expressed their deepest thoughts and feelings through poetry. Poems such as Ode to Autumn by John Keats, Daffodils by William Wordsworth and Song of Myself by Walt Whitman are all-time classics many of us will have studied (and maybe memorized) at school.

Even if you don't aspire to that exalted level, writing poems can still be a hugely satisfying and creative pastime, with therapeutic benefits as well. Writing poetry can also help you improve your written and spoken English generally.

You don't have to write about matters of global significance. Indeed, it's often better to focus on something very specific: a rusty farm gate, for example, or the moment of parting with an old friend. Poetry frequently works best when it encapsulates a particular place or moment and invites readers to draw their own conclusions about its deeper meaning.

One decision you will need to make before you start a poem is the form it will take. There are lots of traditional poetic forms you can use, from sonnets and villanelles to the less formal limericks and ballads. You can also, of course, write in free verse without any formal structure. But many people find that writing poems in a set form is a stimulating challenge, and when it works well gives the poem an added resonance.

Writing a Haiku

A haiku is a form of traditional Japanese poetry. In English it is written in three lines with 5, 7 and 5 syllables. A haiku normally focuses on a single thought or image, and many are written to celebrate nature. Here's an example by Basho Matsuo, a 17th century master of haiku.

An old silent pond...
A frog jumps into the pond,
splash! Silence again.

If you are new to writing poetry, haiku can be a great way to get started. And because these poems are so short, it won't usually take you very long to produce one!

More Tips

• Read a mixture of traditional and modern poetry. Try to attend some live poetry readings as well.

• Use literary devices such as similes and metaphors in your poems, as long as they are original and contribute to the impression you want to convey.

• Read your poems out loud to yourself – this will help you see ways they could be improved.

• Revise and polish your work until it is as good as you can make it. Even the greatest poets don't get everything right first time.

• Join a local writers' group or poets' group. You can get feedback from other members, and hearing their poems may give you fresh insights into your own work.

• If there isn't a group near you (or even if there is) join an online writers' group as well. The forum myWritersCircle.com is free to join and has a section devoted to writing poetry.

• As you improve, consider entering your poems in contests or submitting them for possible inclusion in anthologies. You're unlikely to make a fortune from this, but any successes you achieve will demonstrate that others appreciate your work as well.

#44 CLIMB A MOUNTAIN

Budget: $$$ Time: 🕐🕐🕐🕐🕐

Mountain climbing can be an exhilarating extreme sport, or simply a healthy outdoor challenge. At one extreme are the most challenging climbs such as The Matterhorn in Switzerland and Mount Annapurna in Nepal. These mountains take several days to climb and require specialist gear and careful preparation. They are obviously only suitable for the most experienced climbers.

On the other hand, there are lots of mountains that are less tall and steep and can be climbed (or walked) in a single day with no more than ordinary hiking gear. Some examples include Mount Davidson in San Francisco (really just a short hike) and Mount Snowdon in Wales. If you want to try mountain climbing, these would be good places to start, and if you enjoy yourself, plenty more challenging peaks await.

Equipment

For basic mountain climbing, the most important thing you will require is a strong pair of boots to support your feet and ankles. If you will be traveling on snow or ice you will also need crampons. These fit on and around your boots and provide extra grip. They are made of steel or aluminum.

You will also need warm clothing, including socks, gloves and balaclavas. Temperatures generally fall as you get higher up, so aim to take layers you can put on as required. Waterproofs are an obvious necessity, and you will want a lightweight backpack to carry everything. Other items you will need to take include a map and compass, cell phone (in case you get into difficulties), food and drink, and sunscreen and sunglasses.

Serious mountaineers need a lot of additional kit as well, including ropes, ice picks, karabiners, harnesses, and so on. Casual climbers are unlikely to need all this initially, but if you get into the sport it is something you will need to consider.

<u>More Tips</u>

• Ensure you are fit enough for the climb you are contemplating. Mountain climbing requires physical strength and endurance. Exercises such as running and lifting weights can help with this.

• Some mountains require a permit to climb. Be sure to check in advance and obtain any necessary permissions in good time.

• Keep hydrated. Cold weather can fool people into thinking they're not thirsty, but the cold and high activity level in mountain climbing mean it's important to keep up your fluids at all times.

• Climb in a group, and on more challenging routes with experienced climbers. Never climb alone.

• Let someone know where you are going beforehand, and roughly what time you expect to be back.

• Join a mountain climbing club. Their experienced members will be able to offer invaluable advice on equipment, training, technique, and so on.

• Don't attempt any challenging mountain climb until you have good, solid experience with lesser mountains.

#45 BAKE YOUR OWN BREAD

Budget: $$$ Time: 🕐🕐🕐🕐🕐

Baking bread is a very satisfying thing to do: the smell and taste of freshly baked bread is hard to beat. Indeed, it's no surprise that people trying to sell their home are often advised to have bread baking when potential buyers come to view!

Anyone can make bread with just a few inexpensive ingredients that you probably have in stock already. Here is a simple recipe for making a basic white bread:

Ingredients

1 tablespoon white sugar
2 ½ teaspoons yeast
1 cup lukewarm water

2 ½ cups all-purpose flour
1 teaspoon salt
2 tablespoons olive oil

Method

1. Proof the yeast: Combine the sugar and yeast in a large measuring cup. Add the lukewarm water and stir to combine. Allow the mixture to stand until bubbles are forming on the surface, about five to ten minutes.

2. Combine the flour and salt in a medium-sized bowl. Add the yeast mixture to the flour mixture, and stir well with a wooden spoon.

3. Sprinkle some flour on your worktop. Empty the dough onto this and start kneading it. Add more flour as required to stop the dough sticking. Knead for a couple of minutes, stopping when the dough forms a cohesive mass, then shape it into a ball.

4. Place the dough in an oiled bowl and cover it with a kitchen towel. Allow the dough to rise until it has doubled in size. In a warm kitchen this will take one to two hours.

5. Knead the dough on your worktop a second time, incorporating the olive oil. Work it until it becomes smooth and elastic.

6. Shape the dough into a loaf and place it in an oiled loaf pan. Cover with plastic wrap and allow the dough to rise a second time in a warm, dry place. Once the dough has expanded over the top of the pan, remove the plastic wrap. While the dough is rising, preheat the oven to 350°F (180°C).

7. Bake for 40 minutes, or until the top is golden brown. Allow to cool before turning the bread out of the pan.

8. Serve your bread with butter and jam, or slice it into sandwich bread. Enjoy!

For extra flavor, you can let the bread proof in your refrigerator overnight (see Step 4, above). This is a long, slow fermentation, and will also give the bread a nice crust. Let it come back to room temperature before you begin the second knead.

There are, of course, lots of other bread recipes you can try as well, using different types of flour and other ingredients such as cinnamon and raisins. For a huge range of bread recipes, check out the website http://allrecipes. com/recipes/bread/.

Finally, it's also possible to buy bread-making machines. These can cut down the time required to make bread, and eliminate the need for kneading. You can also set most machines using a timer, so that freshly baked bread is available when you wake up in the morning or get home at night. However, it is absolutely not necessary to have a machine in order to make bread.

#46 GO CYCLING

Budget: $$$ **Time:** 🕐🕐🕐🕐🕐

Be honest – when did you last go out on your bicycle? If it's been a while, why not wheel it out of the shed today and take it for a spin?

You don't have to cycle vast distances. Even a mile or two can give you some welcome fresh air and exercise, and a change of scene from the inside of your living room.

Especially if you haven't ridden your bike for a while, it's important to perform a few safety checks before setting out. Most importantly, check the brakes are working correctly. If you can pull the brake lever until it almost touches the handlebar grip, then you need to tighten the cable. The brake cable can be adjusted near the handlebars.

It's also important to check tire pressures. Proper tire pressure lets your bike roll quickly, ride smoothly, and fend off flats. Narrow tires need more pressure than wide ones. Road tires typically require 80 to 130 psi, mountain tires 30 to 50 psi, and hybrid tires 50 to 70 psi. To find your ideal pressure, start in the middle of these ranges, then factor in your body weight. The more you weigh, the higher the tire pressure needs to be. For example, if a 160-pound cyclist uses 100 psi on his road bike, a 200-pound cyclist should run closer to 120 psi, while a 130-pound cyclist could get away with 80 psi. Never go above or below the manufacturer's recommended pressures.

More Tips

• Adjust the saddle of your bike to the correct height. To find this, take off your shoes, sit on your bike (leaning against a wall), push the pedal to 6 o'clock and place your heel on it. Adjust the saddle until your leg is straight. This will translate into a very slight bend of the knee when you are cycling.

• Don't wait until you're on the road to hone your flat-changing skills. Practice changing a tire at home using the same pump and tools you carry on your ride, and you'll be less worried about getting a flat while you're out.

• Lubricate the chain with cycle oil regularly, and especially if you start to hear squeaky noises. Apply oil to the entire length of the chain as you turn the pedal backward.

• Always wear a cycle helmet. In the event of an accident this can protect you from serious injury.

• Check your tires for cuts and excessive wear once a month, and replace them if necessary.

• Cycling is great on your own, but it's even more fun with family and friends. Just be sure to keep an eye out for traffic, and don't ride side-by-side on busy roads.

Finally, if you have an old bicycle and you're unsure whether it is safe, get it checked over by a professional before taking it for a ride. A bike shop mechanic will be able to advise you whether it's cheaper to get your bike fixed or buy a new one.

#47 START A PART-TIME BUSINESS

Budget: $$$ Time: 🕐🕐🕐🕐🕐

We could all do with a bit of extra cash, so why not switch off the TV and do something more remunerative instead?

As well as the financial benefits, many people find that running a part-time, home-based business is a stimulating challenge, helps them meet new people, and can provide a lot of creative satisfaction too. Plus, in these uncertain times, it is never a bad thing to have an extra string to your bow!

There are many different ways you can make money from home. Here are five ideas to start you thinking:

Freelance Writing

Lots of people write in their spare time. Although it's competitive, there is big money to be made in this field. Many people get started by writing articles for magazines, newspapers and websites. Think about your areas of special interest and experience, and contact publishers with ideas (and outlines) for articles you could write for them.

Proofreading

Or if you're good at spotting the mistakes other people make, proofreading may appeal. Freelance proofreaders typically work for publishing houses, though they may also be hired directly by writers. You will need a high standard of written English and a knowledge of the special proofreading marks (easy to learn online or from books). Your chances of getting work will be greater if you have completed an accredited training course.

Online Auction Trading

This is a hugely popular home-based business idea. You could start by selling things you have lying around at home that you no longer need. Once you have done that, you could graduate to buying products cheaply from wholesalers, second-hand stores, and so on, and sell them on eBay or other online auction sites for profit.

Affiliate Marketing

This is another popular online business opportunity. As an affiliate marketer you promote other companies' products and services and receive a commission for any sales that result. To get into affiliate marketing you will need some website building skills, but it's easy enough to learn the basics (which is really all that is required).

Children's Party Planning

If you like kids, this could be for you. Many parents will spend big bucks to throw a great birthday party for their child. While they could just organize a party at home, many people don't have the time or energy to pull it off. That's where a party business comes in. There's a demand for people who can arrange the whole event, mail the invitations, stock the goody bags and arrange discounts with local venues. Parents are often willing to pay handsomely for this – and of course events will be mainly at the weekends, so they need not clash with your main job (if you have one).

There are lots of other possibilities as well – take a look at www.entrepreneur.com/homebasedbiz for more ideas and inspiration. Just remember to research your home-business idea carefully, fulfil any legal requirements (e.g. registering with the tax authorities), and then go for it. Who knows, you could end up with a whole new career!

#48 SEE SOME LIVE THEATER

Budget: $$$ Time: ①①①①①

If you live near a big city, you will be spoiled for choice as far as live shows are concerned. But almost anywhere, there will be regional, local and community theaters, often offering great entertainment at a fraction of the price of a ticket on Broadway!

There are lots of different types of show, so whatever your taste there is likely to be something to interest you. They include 'classic' plays by authors such as Shakespeare and Tennessee Williams, but also plays by contemporary authors that address modern-day issues. As well as serious plays, there are of course comedies. Another hugely popular option is the musical, where as well as a story to enjoy, you get music, singing and dancing as well.

Before going to any theater show, it's important to do a bit of preliminary research to check what it is about and whether you think it would appeal to you. Read listings magazines and newspapers, and check out the theater (or theater company's) website. It's also a good idea to seek out independent reviews. Don't take everything you read in a review as gospel – it's just one person's opinion, after all – but if all the reviews are negative you might want to look elsewhere.

More Tips

• In New York and London there are discount booths where you can often buy last-minute tickets cheaply. The StubHub website at StubHub.com and StubHub.co.uk is also well worth trying.

• Many theaters now let you book online and print your own ticket, which is obviously quick and convenient. If possible, choose your own seat rather than selecting the 'best available' option. The system's idea of what is best may be very different from yours!

#49 BLOW SOAP BUBBLES

Budget: $$$ Time: 🕐🕐🕐🕐🕐

Who doesn't enjoy blowing soap bubbles on a warm sunny day? Obviously this is perfect if you have young children, but if not it's still a great opportunity to get in touch with your inner child!

To make your bubble solution, combine 15 parts water with one part liquid dish detergent (baby shampoo also works well). For best results try to use soft water. If the water that comes out of your faucet is hard, filter it or use the distilled water that is sold for use with steam irons.

If you want the bubbles to last longer, you can try adding a thickener such as glycerin, sugar or corn syrup. Be careful, though, as adding too much will make the suds too heavy for bubble formation. Using a wooden spoon, stir the solution gently in a large bowl or pan, and take it outside.

You will also need something to blow your bubbles from. One low-cost idea is to take a wire coat hanger and twist it into a loop. You can even make it heart-shaped, square or other shapes, if you're clever enough to bend it well. Plastic six-pack rings can make excellent bubble wands as well.

Another possibility is to take tin cans or cartons, remove the tops and bottoms, and flatten any sharp metal edges. Just dip the ends into the solution and wave them in the air.

For creating bigger bubbles, try making a paper bubble cone. Roll up a piece of paper into a cone shape and trim the larger end to be smooth. Dip this end into the bubble solution, allowing it to soak in for half a minute the first time. Then blow gently into the smaller end. Lots of bubble solution gets stored in the layers of paper, leading to giant-sized bubbles.

#50 LEARN FIRST AID +

Budget: $$$ Time: ◷◷◷◷◷

Learning first aid is one of the most worthwhile things you can do. Taking appropriate action promptly when accidents or other traumas occur can be invaluable to a victim.

You can pick up the basics of first aid from books and websites (e.g. RedCross. org), but to learn life-saving techniques such as CPR (cardiopulmonary resuscitation) there's no substitute for attending a course. Introductory classes are often provided by schools and employers. You may also be able to book onto a more advanced training course such as those offered by the Red Cross, which can lead to certification in the relevant skills.

One basic first aid principle everyone should know is the Three C's. This is a three-step guide to safely negotiating any emergency situation:

1. Check the Surroundings

Evaluate the situation carefully to see if there is anything that might put you at risk of harm. This might include fire, toxic smoke or gas, an unstable building, live electrical wires, risk of drowning, and so on. Don't rush into a situation where you could end up hurting yourself as well.

If approaching the victim will endanger your life, seek professional help. First aid becomes useless if you can't safely perform it without putting yourself at risk.

2. Call for Help

Call the emergency services immediately if you believe someone to be seriously injured or ill. If you are the only person on the scene, try to establish whether the victim is breathing before calling for help. Don't leave them alone for any extensive length of time.

3. Care for the Person

Caring for someone who has just gone through serious trauma includes both physical treatment and emotional support. Stay calm and try to be reassuring. Let the person know that help is on the way, and that everything will be alright.

4. Create a Home First Aid Kit

A well-stocked first aid kit is an essential for every home. Even if you already have one, it's important to check it regularly to ensure items have not deteriorated or expired.

If you're creating a first aid kit from scratch, store it in a waterproof container (or put the items in zip-lock bags). Separate the contents into two sections, one with basic medical supplies such as bandages and ointments, and the other with important medications for your family.

Fill the box with sterile and/or newly-bought items. These may include:

• adhesive dressings, of various shapes and sizes
• small (but sharp) scissors
• gauze pads of various sizes (though you can always cut them if necessary)
• surgical tape
• cotton balls, or maxi pads
• a thermometer
• tweezers for pulling out splinters
• a bee-sting kit
• sterile dressings
• roller bandages
• antibiotic ointment
• latex gloves to protect yourself from the bodily fluids of others.

Home first aid kits are best kept in the kitchen, rather than the bathroom, where high moisture levels can cause items to deteriorate faster. It's also a good idea to carry a first aid kit in the car, and take one on trips away too.

Learning a few basic skills and preparing a first aid kit could save the life of a loved one in future. It's got to be worth skipping a few episodes of a reality show for!

#51 JOIN (OR START) A SOCIAL CLUB

Budget: $$$ Time: ◷◷◷◷◷

Joining a social club can be a great way to meet new friends, share hobbies and interests, and discover new ones!

Many social clubs are based round a particular activity, from stamp collecting to modern jazz. Others are broader-based, perhaps aimed at people living in a certain area, working in a particular field, or just within a certain demographic (eg. local entrepreneurs).

Most social clubs charge a modest membership to cover their costs, though some are free. Typically they organize a variety of events, from restaurant nights and quizzes to theater trips and sporting challenges. Many clubs have a high proportion of single members, but apart from those targeted specifically at single folk (or men/women only) they all welcome couples as well.

If you're not sure what clubs are in your area, a good place to look is the website Meetup.com. Enter your nearest city in the search box and the distance you are willing to travel (e.g. 25 miles). The site will show you all the clubs in that area, including how many members they have and the date of their next meeting. You can get more information and ask to join by clicking on the name of the group concerned.

Starting Your Own Club

If there is nothing that immediately appeals to you locally, it's very easy to start your own social club. Here's a three-step plan.

1. Start by deciding the theme around which your club will be based. As mentioned above, it could be people who share a common interest or work in a particular industry. Or it could just be for people who are new to your city and want to make more friends.

2. Many clubs start with a small group of friends or colleagues. If you know two or three people who share your interest, arrange a time and place where you can meet (e.g. a coffee shop). If it goes well and you have fun, arrange another meeting in a week or two. Invite everyone to bring along a like-minded friend.

3. Set up a page for your club on Facebook and maybe a Twitter account as well. This can be great for keeping in touch with club members and attracting new ones. Be sure to list your club at Meetup.com as well, and consider putting up fliers locally.

More Tips

• Starting a social club from scratch can be hard work but also very rewarding. You'll need to be friendly and reasonably outgoing, in order to make new members feel welcome.

• Don't be disappointed if some people stop attending. This can happen for all sorts of reasons that may be nothing to do with you or your group.

• Encourage existing members to recruit friends and colleagues by telling them how great the club is.

• Keep the tone of meetings light and informal. Many people are put off by clubs that appear excessively bureaucratic.

• Aim to create a program of events over the coming months to build interest and keep people coming back for more.

#52 GO FOR A SWIM

Budget: $$$ Time: 🕐🕐🕐🕐🕐

Swimming is a wonderful activity for people of all ages, both relaxing and invigorating.

It also has many health benefits. Swimming works the whole of your body, but without putting any part of it under excess strain. It's therefore an ideal way to exercise stiff muscles and sore joints, especially if you're overweight or suffer from arthritis.

Swimming tones your body – when did you last see a flabby dolphin? – and because it's an aerobic exercise, it will help strengthen your heart. Swimming is also recognized as one of the best calorie burners around, so it's great for keeping your weight under control. What more persuasion do you need?!

There are public swimming pools in most large towns and cities (and many smaller ones as well). Most charge a modest entry fee, but some are free. There are also often discounts for children, the unemployed, students and senior citizens.

Another option if you live near the coast is swimming in the sea. Many people especially enjoy this, as the salt content in sea water gives added buoyancy, while the rocking motion of the waves provides an added dimension. You could also put on a snorkel mask and explore the marine life below you. Just be sure to check that the area is safe, and avoid going out of your depth if you are not a confident swimmer.

Finally, another option growing in popularity is open water swimming. This is where you swim in lakes, rivers, natural pools, and so on. Open water swimming can be exciting and exhilarating, and of course it is free! However, it's important to check that the water in question is safe for swimming. There will be no lifeguard keeping watch over you either – so once you're in, be aware of everything going on around, including boats, other swimmers, wildlife, and so on. Keep an eye on the weather too, and if you hear thunder, get to shore and a safe environment immediately. Finally, never go open water swimming on your own. The risk is just too great.

Learning to Swim

If you can't swim, why not make this the year you learn? You're never too old to learn, and as well as being a healthy and relaxing pastime, the ability to swim could save your life (or that of a loved one) someday.

Most public pools offer lessons for children and adults, so ask at reception what is available. You can book lessons once a week, but a popular option nowadays is an intensive course, where you go every day for a week or so. These courses can work particularly well, as there is less time to forget what you learned the last time!

Finally, if you need to save money you may have a friend who would be willing to teach you. Be careful, though, as not everyone has the patience or communication skills to make a good teacher. It is really best to learn the basics from an accredited swimming coach, and then practice with a friend who can support and encourage you, and will be there to help if you get into difficulties.

#53 LEARN TO KNIT

Budget: $$$ Time: ⏰⏰⏰⏰⏰

In recent years knitting has been growing in popularity. Many people find it a satisfying, relaxing activity, and of course you end up with a useful garment as well, either to wear yourself or give to a friend.

Knitting is an inexpensive hobby. All you need initially are knitting needles and some suitable yarn, along with a sharp pair of scissors. A darning or tapestry needle is useful for some purposes as well.

So far as knitting needles are concerned, it's important to choose a pair you find comfortable that are also suitable for the project you have in mind. Needles are made from many materials, the most popular being bamboo, wood, plastic, and aluminum. Beginners are generally advised to choose needles that are not so slippery they cause the yarn to slip off. Bamboo and wood can be good choices, while metal needles tend to be more suitable for experienced knitters.

You also have a wide choice of yarns. As well as the color, you will need to decide whether you want the article to be washable, to keep you warm in cold weather, or to be dressy enough for formal wear. In addition, if you are knitting for someone else, you need to take into account any allergies they may have. Quite a few people are allergic to wool, for example.

Learning the Stitches

This is, of course, fundamental to knitting. As a beginner you will need to learn how to make a slip knot (this will be your first stitch), how to cast on (add more beginning stitches to your needle), and how to do both knit stitches and purl stitches. Finally, once your piece is finished, you will need to be able to 'cast off' to create a flat, finished edge to your project. You can learn these techniques at a class or from a knitting website (see below).

There are many other techniques and stitches you can learn too, but once you can master the basics mentioned above, you will be all set to start your first project.

More Tips

• Steer clear of fluffy or decorative yarns as a novice knitter. They may look attractive, but if you make any mistakes with that type of yarn it won't be easy to tell.

• Count the stitches on every row carefully. If you have more on some rows than others, the end result will be uneven and disappointing.

• If it's your first time knitting, it's better to use a thick yarn and bigger needles, as it takes less time to knit a project.

• Try not to make your stitching too tight, so you can fit the needle through easily.

• Practice your knitting regularly, to ensure you don't forget how to do it.

Finally, as mentioned above, there are many excellent free resources online to help you learn to knit. A great place to start is http://knitting.about.com. As well as links to illustrated tutorials and videos, there are easy knitting patterns you can download free for items such as headbands and baby blankets.

#54 LEARN A LANGUAGE

Budget: $$$ Time: 🕐🕐🕐🕐🕐

Learning a language is a fascinating challenge and a great way to keep your brain active (much better than watching TV!).

There are many other potential benefits too. Speaking another language can boost your career prospects considerably. Or there may be a particular country you like to visit on vacation, in which case learning their language will give you added enjoyment.

And finally, many of us have colleagues, friends and relatives who are not native English speakers, so learning their language can help us communicate with and understand them better.

What Language?

This is clearly a personal choice. If you have roots in another country, for example, learning that language would obviously hold special appeal. On the other hand, if you hope to improve your employability, a widely spoken language such as Spanish or Chinese (Mandarin) might be your best bet.

A further consideration is how easy the language is to learn. The Defense Language Institute in Monterey, California, divides the languages they teach into four groups, from easiest to most difficult, as measured by how long it takes to bring students (mainly native English speakers) to a certain level of proficiency. These are listed below, from 1 (least difficult) to 4 (most difficult).

1. Afrikaans, Danish, Dutch, French, Haitian Creole, Italian, Norwegian, Portuguese, Romanian, Spanish, Swahili, Swedish
2. Bulgarian, Dari, Farsi (Persian), German, (Modern) Greek, Hindi-Urdu, Indonesian, Malay

3. Amharic, Bengali, Burmese, Czech, Finnish, (Modern) Hebrew, Hungarian, Khmer (Cambodian), Lao, Nepali, Pilipino (Tagalog), Polish, Russian, Serbo-Croatian, Sinhala, Thai, Tamil, Turkish, Vietnamese
4. Arabic, Chinese, Japanese, Korean

Ways to Learn

Classes are one possibility, but an hour or two a week isn't ideal, as you will typically forget much of what you learn between lessons. A better option is an intensive course, where you are immersed in the language for anywhere from a few weeks to six months. Such courses are run by colleges, universities, and private training companies.

A more flexible (and probably less expensive) option is a multimedia training course. A huge range of courses is available to buy on CD, DVD, and – increasingly – online. One of the best-known providers is Rosetta Stone, who have a website at RosettaStone.com. There are also free online language training websites, such as LearnaLanguage.com and Duolingo. com.

The Learning Process

If you have chosen a language such as Russian, Chinese or Japanese, your first step will be learning the alphabet they use. Russian can be particularly challenging, as some letters such as P, B and H represent different sounds than in English.

After that, most courses focus on building vocabulary alongside basic grammar, so you can start constructing simple sentences.

For getting fluent, though, there is no substitute for regular practice. Holding conversations with native speakers is ideal. If you don't know anyone locally, the website LiveMocha.com will connect you with people who will converse with you in their language in exchange for letting them practice their English with you. It can also help to watch movies and TV shows in the language you are learning, read popular magazines and newspapers, and so on.

Good luck, bonne chance, and buona fortuna!

#55 GROW YOUR OWN VEGETABLES

Budget: $$$ Time: ⏱⏱⏱⏱⏱

What could be better than growing your own vegetables? Home-grown vegetables are as fresh as they can possibly be, with all the taste and health benefits this brings. Not only that, you can save money on your weekly shop.

Even if you don't have a garden, you can grow many vegetables on your window-sill or in pots or baskets outside. Here are some favorite vegetables to start you off:

Tomatoes

Tomatoes are a cook's staple, as well as being delicious alone or in salads. And the good news is that they are easy to cultivate as well. You can grow them from seed or buy small plants from garden centers. There are many different varieties, including some that do well in tubs and hanging baskets, and others that grow vigorously in greenhouses or outdoors. Tomatoes need full sun to thrive. They need watering regularly, and should be fed a special tomato food during the growing season.

Zucchini

Also known as courgettes, these vegetables are a main ingredient in ratatouille as well as many other Mediterranean dishes. They grow well outside in warmer climates, or in a greenhouse. Like tomatoes, they also do well in growbags. They need a sunny spot and plenty of watering. To keep plants productive you will need to harvest them at least once a week at the height of the season. Once they're around 10 cm, use a sharp knife to cut the vegetable from the plant.

Potatoes

It's only when you've tasted home-grown potatoes you realize how inferior most shop bought ones are! It's best to buy seed potatoes from garden centers, but you can also use other potatoes that have started to sprout. Plant your potatoes in a patch of land, or in a planter on your patio. Ensure the soil is as weed-free as possible, and add some compost or manure to make it nutrient-rich. You will know your potatoes are ready to harvest when the leaves turn yellow and start to wither.

Chili Peppers

Chili peppers are easy to grow indoors on a sunny windowsill, and great to have in the kitchen if you like spicy food. You can either grow them from seed or buy plants from garden centers. Chili peppers need plenty of warm sunshine but must be kept out of draughts. Water them regularly and give them a monthly feed with a liquid fertilizer. Harvest them one at a time, using shears or scissors to snip the stem directly above the pepper.

There are many other vegetables you can grow at home as well – other possibilities include cucumbers, eggplants (also called aubergines), peas, beans, radishes, lettuces, squash, and many more.

When you grow your own vegetables, you will be feeding your family healthier and less-expensive foods that will give them the nutrients they need, while giving you hours of fresh air and light exercise in the garden. Surely that's a much better use of your time than watching TV!

#56 PLAY AN ONLINE GAME

Budget: $$$ Time: 🕐🕑🕒🕓🕔

If you haven't yet discovered the joys of online gaming, why not give it a try? Admittedly, you will still be looking at a screen, but instead of being a passive consumer, you'll be an active participant!

Online gaming nowadays is hugely popular, and it's by no means limited to shoot 'em ups targeted at teenage boys. Some of the most popular games require creativity and good communication skills, rather than just fast reaction times.

Most online games can be played on games consoles such as the Xbox and PlayStation, but many can also be played on a tablet, smartphone or desktop PC. Some are entirely free, some require an initial payment followed by a subscription, and others simply require a one-time payment.

An example of the latter is the hugely popular Minecraft, which recently topped 50 million users. In this game players take on the role of architects, building anything from simple huts to amazingly elaborate castles and resorts in an almost infinite landscape. You can work on your own, but many people choose to collaborate on larger projects with other players. Minecraft is not competitive – the rewards come from building something amazing and beautiful that other players will visit and admire. You can find out more about Minecraft and try it out for free at Minecraft.net.

There are many other online games as well. One is Neverwinter (www.playneverwinter.com), a popular 'Dungeons and Dragons' fantasy adventure game which is entirely free. Another is World of Warcraft (http://us.battle.net/wow), a multiplayer online game very popular among women as well as men. You can play the starter edition free, but if you want to move on, payment is by subscription.

#57 TAKE IN A MOVIE

Budget: $$$ Time: ○○○○○

Yes, you can always watch a movie on TV, but how much better to see them on the big screen they were designed for.

A trip to the cinema can make a highly enjoyable and inexpensive outing, whether it's on your own, with a friend, or the while family.

Your first step will be researching what's on. You can find this information in local newspapers and listings magazines, and on the internet. Most cinemas nowadays have websites. Just search for cinema (or movie theater) and the name of your town or city, and the relevant website should be displayed.

For what to see, most people are guided by reviews and, of course, the recommendations of friends and relatives. Again, you can find reviews of the latest movies in newspapers and magazines and on the internet. Always bear in mind that any review is only one person's opinion. However, if everyone agrees that a certain film is a stinker, you might prefer to opt for something else instead.

Often it is possible to book tickets online, and if you can it is well worth doing, as it will save you queuing at the venue.

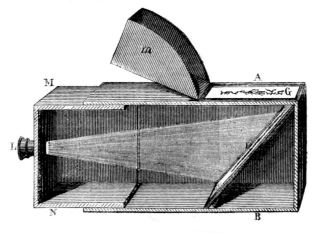

#58 BAKE YOUR OWN COOKIES

Budget: $$$	Time: 🕐🕐🕐🕐🕐

OK, they may not be the healthiest of snacks, but everyone loves freshly-baked cookies, and they smell delicious as well.

You can of course buy cookie mix from shops and supermarkets, but it's easy (and very cheap) to make your own from a few basic ingredients, and you can then adjust the recipe to suit your personal taste.

Here's a basic recipe for chocolate chip cookies to start you off:

Ingredients

2 1/4 cups flour
1 teaspoon salt
1 teaspoon baking soda
1 cup butter, softened but not melted

3/4 cup packed brown sugar
3/4 cup granulated sugar
2 large eggs
1 teaspoon vanilla extract
1 to 2 cups chocolate chips

Method

1. Preheat your oven to 375°F (190°C).

2. In a medium-sized bowl, combine the flour, salt, and baking soda, adding them through a sieve to avoid any lumps. Gently mix, then set the bowl aside.

3. In a separate large bowl, beat the butter and sugars together, then beat in the eggs and vanilla. Stir until they are all completely combined.

4. Slowly add the dry ingredients from the medium bowl to the wet ingredients in the large bowl, then add the chocolate chips. Mix and stir until the ingredients are fully combined. At this point you should have a moderately thick cookie dough.

5. Drop spoonfuls of the dough onto a pre-greased or lined baking sheet. Leave at least an inch of space between the cookies, as they will spread out when they cook.

6. Bake for about 10 minutes. Remove the pan from the oven and let the cookies rest there for 3–4 minutes.

7. Using a spatula, lift the cookies off and place them on wax paper or a cooling rack. Allow them to cool for a further five minutes.

8. Enjoy your cookies when hot and steamy, or cooled and slightly crisp. They will go perfectly with a cup of tea or a glass of milk!

<u>More Tips</u>

• Don't over-stir the dough or it will turn to brick. Add the dry ingredients gradually, but in no more than four or five batches.

• If you don't have any chocolate chips, a good alternative would be a bar of chocolate snapped into little pieces.

• Watch your cookies while they are in the oven to ensure they don't start to burn.

• Experiment by adding other ingredients, such as raisins and other dried fruit, cocoa powder, coconut and peanut butter (not all at once, though!).

• If you want to make your cookies a bit healthier, you could use whole wheat flour and substitute an artificial sweetener such as Splenda for some or all of the sugar. You can also reduce the fat content by using a trans-fat-free margarine or vegetable oil.

• Making cookies is a great project for children to help with, but make sure they don't burn themselves. Putting the cookies in and out of the oven is best done by an adult wearing protective mitts.

For additional inspiration, there are lots of cookie recipes on the internet. For starters, check out http://allrecipes.com/recipes/desserts/cookies/ and http://smittenkitchen.com/cookie-recipes/. Have fun, but don't eat too many!

#59 HOLD A GARAGE SALE

Budget: $$$ Time: 🕐🕐🕐🕐🕐

A garage sale (or yard sale) is a great way to clear out the clutter in your home and turn it into cash.

Start by gathering items to sell. Look in the attic, shed and garage, then go from room to room, identifying things you no longer need. If you haven't used something for over a year, it's a good sign you won't miss it!

List each item and the price you want for it. You will be labelling everything anyway, but it is best to have a master list too, as labels have a habit of going astray. Try to set prices people will regard as good value without being a complete giveaway.

Attach a clearly written price label to each item. You can purchase adhesive labels, or you can be more professional and use a 'sticker gun'. If you have a number of similar items all priced the same (e.g. books), don't bother pricing them individually. Place them all in a box, and label the box.

Choose a day for your sale when fine weather is forecast, preferably at the weekend. Put a notice outside your home saying 'Garage Sale Here Today – Bargains Galore!' or some such. You could also list your sale free of charge at GarageSaleFinder.com or GarageSaleFinder.co.uk.

Other promotional possibilities include handing out fliers and putting up cards on community noticeboards. Finally, don't forget to invite your friends and neighbors, and ask them to spread the word as well!

On the day, set up in good time and ensure your goods are attractively displayed. Have a secure cash box with plenty of change, and keep a close watch on it at all times. Have help available from family members or friends, so you can take a break occasionally. At the end, offer last-minute deals on any items that have failed to sell.

#60 GO TO A FARMERS' MARKET

Budget: $$$ Time: 🕐🕐🕐🕐🕐

In recent years farmers' markets (also called greenmarkets) have been springing up everywhere. As the name indicates, they are places where farmers sell their products directly to the public.

There are many advantages to shopping at a farmers' market. As well as great-value prices, you will be getting ultra-fresh produce crammed with vitamins and other nutrients, which has been grown (or reared) locally. You may also be able to buy products that simply aren't available in shops and supermarkets, such as artisan bread and cheeses, hand-harvested honey, and so on.

In addition, you will be supporting your local farmers, who will receive all the money you pay for the produce, rather than the small percentage (typically under a third) they get from the supermarkets.

Some farmers' markets are open every day, but many only operate once a week or once a month. Check in your local newspaper or listings magazine to find out about markets in your area. You can also search online for 'famers market' plus the name of your town or city. There are also websites that promote and publicize farmers' markets, including LocalHarvest.org, Localfoods.org.uk, and Farmersmarketsintheusa.com.

More Tips

• Know what's in season, as such produce will generally be available at the best prices and the highest quality. Ask the vendors about any other products that will be coming to market soon.

• On the other hand, for the best bargains, go at the end. Farmers and other vendors often prefer to discount products rather than having to load them up and take them home again.

#61 HAVE A BARBECUE

Budget: $$$ Time: 🕐🕐🕐🕐🕐

Everyone loves a barbecue. So if the sun's shining, why not stock up with food and drink, light up the grill, and invite all your friends and neighbors round!

Although gas barbecues are easy, cheap and convenient, nothing beats the flavor of food cooked on a charcoal grill. There are at least two reasons for this…

• Charcoal grills get much hotter, and are great for searing meat in particular.
• The woodsmoke imparts far more flavor.

But the choice is yours, of course!

One tip when cooking meat is to use thicker cuts. This is because thicker cuts give more of the perfect barbecue combination: crispy, seared outside and a tender, juicy inside. A thicker steak, for example, has time to develop a nice brown sear while the inside of the steak cooks. A simple rule of thumb is to buy steaks that are between 1–2 inches thick.

Sausages and burgers are barbecue essentials. You can also cook veggie burgers, but try to get the sort that keep their shape when cooking and don't simply disintegrate on the grill. Soy and Quorn burgers can work well, or you can make your own, of course.

Fish can also be delicious on a barbecue. If you can get it, swordfish is a perfect barbecue food, as it holds up well and doesn't flake apart like more delicate fish. Sear it over medium to high heat for a short time on one side and an even shorter time on the other, being careful not to overcook.

Vegetables cook quickly and are delicious with a hint of smoke from the grill. Just toss them in a little oil beforehand to stop them drying out.

Finally, fruit can be cooked on the barbecue as well. Most fruit cooks very quickly, so wait until the barbecue has cooled down a little. You can then cook pieces of fruit on kebabs, marinaded in melted butter, lemon juice and sugar, and served with ice cream. The ideal barbecue dessert!

More Tips

• Stick to simple seasonings. Most of the time, all you really need are salt and pepper.

• Prepare a big bowl of salad to accompany the meat and fish, and plenty of fresh crusty bread as well.

• Give the barbecue a quick clean before using it and a more thorough one afterward (once it has cooled). Use a putty knife and wire-bristle brush to clean food and debris from the tops and bottoms of grates or rods, and use a scraper on solid grill panels.

• Always be safety conscious at a barbecue. Keep children well away from hot coals or gas, and wear an apron and a mitt to protect your hands.

• Check that meat is thoroughly cooked inside and out. Use a food thermometer to check that it has reached a safe minimum internal temperature. The USDA Food Safety and Inspection Service recommends at least 145°F (63°C) for most meats and 165°F (74°C) for poultry. Allow it to rest for at least three minutes before eating.

• Never use gasoline as a fire-starter or accelerant, as this can cause explosions.

#62 BECOME AN EXTRA

Budget: $$$ Time: 🕐🕐🕐🕐🕐

Instead of watching celebs on the box, why not sign up as a film or TV extra and maybe meet them face to face? As an extra, you'll make some money, get a chance to see how movies and TV shows are made, and perhaps become immortalized on screen.

In principle, almost anyone can become an extra. Obviously, it will help if you live near a film or TV studio, or a popular location for filming. Many gigs are for a single day, but occasionally they can go on for a week or longer. Some extras in long-running TV serials continue to work on the show over a period of years.

Contrary to what you might think, you don't have to be ultra-attractive to be an extra. Indeed, that can be a drawback. Extras are generally required for crowd scenes or to provide background, e.g. as the main actors hold a conversation in a bar. In most cases extras are expected to look average and normal (for whatever may be the setting), so they won't distract viewers from the stars.

One thing you do need, however, is stamina. Working as an extra can involve a lot of waiting around, sometimes in cramped, uncomfortable conditions, or in the open air exposed to the weather. You may be required to stand, sit, or repeat some motion for hours on end, until the director is finally satisfied with the shot. A typical working day is 10–12 hours, and on a music video it can be even longer.

How To Get Work

It's possible to get work applying directly to TV and film production companies, but most people get into this business by joining a casting agency.

In the US, the best-known is Central Casting, which has offices in New York, New Orleans and Los Angeles. You can find out more (and apply) via their website at CentralCasting.com. For film and TV opportunities in the UK, the website FilmExtras.co.uk is a good place to start. Elsewhere, just search online for 'casting agency' plus the name of your nearest city.

Once you are registered with an agency they will keep your details (and photo) on file, and contact you when an opportunity matching your description comes in. You will then receive a call sheet from the production office and told when and where to report.

When you arrive, introduce yourself to whoever is in charge of extras (on a film set this will typically be the second assistant director or extras captain). They will explain what is required of you, so listen carefully and do exactly as you are told. They will be very specific about things like when to come and go, and whom you should and shouldn't speak to. It is, of course, quite likely there will be major stars wandering around, and the last thing they will want you to do is approach them uninvited.

Some extras have been 'discovered' this way and gone on to become big stars in their own right, but the great majority simply enjoy the work and the extra money it brings in. Good luck, and see you in the next blockbuster!

#63 SOLVE A PUZZLE

Budget: $$$ Time: 🕐🕐🕐🕐🕐

Switch off the telly and give your brain a workout with a puzzle!

There is a growing body of evidence that challenging yourself this way can help keep you mentally sharp, and perhaps even roll back the effects of ageing.

There are many different types of puzzle you could try. Here are some of the most popular:

Sudoku – This is a number puzzle. The aim is to fill a 9×9 grid with digits, so that each column and row and each of the nine 3×3 sub-grids contains all the digits from 1 to 9. The puzzle setter provides a partly completed grid, which for a well-posed puzzle will have a unique solution.

Crossword – Crossword puzzles have been around for over 100 years. A crossword is made up of black and white squares and a list of clues, the answer to each of which is a word or phrase. Each clue has a number – for example, '1 Across' or '15 Down'. Straight (or quick) crosswords usually consist of simple word definitions. The more difficult 'cryptic' crosswords also use anagrams and wordplay.

Wordsearch – In this type of puzzle a grid consisting of single letters is provided. This is usually square and around 12x12, though it can be larger or smaller. The aim is to find all the hidden words in the grid, which may be spelled out in any direction, including diagonally. In some puzzles, once all the hidden words have been found, the remaining ones spell out a secret message.

Logic Puzzles – Logic puzzles involve using reasoning and deduction to fully explain a situation from certain information provided. For example, you might be required to work out which of six families live in six houses on a road, from information such as the Browns do not live next door to the Smiths, and the Robinsons share a garden fence with the Carters.

You can find puzzles in all sorts of places. Many newspapers and popular magazines include them, and there are also dedicated magazines for different types of puzzle. You can buy puzzle books and e-books, and there are also free and low-cost smartphone apps (ideal for whiling away a few minutes on the bus or train).

There are also websites that publish puzzles in all these categories. They are generally free, as they are funded by advertising. Here are a few to start you off:

Sudoku – www.sudoku.com, www.websudoku.com, www.dailysudoku.com

Crosswords – www.bestcrosswords.com, http://webcrosswords.com

Wordsearch – www.superwordsearchpuzzles.com, www.puzzles.ca/wordsearch.html

Logic puzzles – www.logic-puzzles.org, www.brainbashers.com/logic

More Tips

• Start with easy puzzles and work your way up to harder ones.

• If you get stuck, put the puzzle to one side and come back to it later. With fresh eyes you will often see an answer that escaped you before.

• For added fun, collaborate with a friend or family member to tackle more challenging puzzles.

• You could also hold puzzle-solving challenges or tournaments with friends and workmates.

#64 GO FLY A KITE

Budget: $$**$ **Time: 🕐🕐🕐🕐🕐

Flying a kite is great fun on a windy day. It will give you fresh air and light exercise, and many people find it very relaxing.

There are many different shapes and sizes of kite you can buy, or you can make your own (see below). The traditional triangular design is still widely used, but modern technology has provided many other options too, including boxes, cylinders, butterflies, bi-planes, and so on. This new diversity has made it not only fun to fly kites but very enjoyable to watch them as well.

Kites come in three main types, single-line, dual-line and quad-line. Single-line kites are the cheapest and simplest, and can often be used straight out of the bag without any adjustment. They come in all shapes and sizes, and are suitable for all ages and levels of experience.

Dual-line kites give you the ability to maneuver your kite in virtually any direction, allowing you to perform loops and other stunts. Landing a dual-line kite takes a bit of practice, but can generally be mastered without too much difficulty.

Finally, quad-line kites give you ultimate control over your kite, and are the type used in competition.

For successful kite-flying you want a breezy day but not gale-force winds. With a light breeze, you can make your kite dance and soar, and maybe even perform loops and tricks. If there are leaves on the ground being tossed around gently, that's perfect. But only fly in safe conditions, when there is no sign of rain or lightning. Wet kite lines can conduct electricity from clouds, potentially causing a lethal electric shock. Benjamin Franklin was lucky to survive his famous experiment!

It's best (and more fun anyway) to have a buddy to assist you when kite flying. One of you can then hold the string, while the other holds – and then releases – the kite. Arrange yourselves so that the wind is blowing from the flier to the launcher. Wait for a suitable gust of wind. The flier should then pull on the string to provide a bit of tension and signal the launcher to release the kite into the air.

More Tips

• For obvious reasons, avoid flying kites near power lines.

• It's also best to avoid flying anywhere near trees or buildings. A kite needs lots of space and moves around a lot on its way up and down.

• Challenge yourself to see how long you can keep your kite in the air. You could also swap roles with your friend to see who is the better flier!

• Once you are confident with your kite-flying, try performing a few stunts (this is easier with a dual- or quad-line kite).

• Bring your camera as well, and take some photos when it's not your turn to fly.

Finally, this article reveals how to make a kite in 17 steps from an old plastic bag: www.wikihow.com/Make-a-Kite-Out-of-a-Plastic-Bag. For more inspiration, just search using the phrase 'make a kite'.

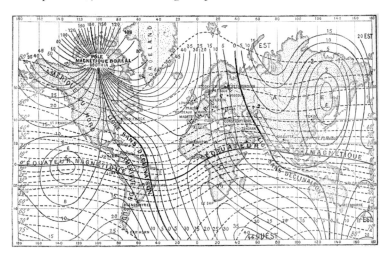

#65 PLAY A CHALK GAME

Budget: $$$ **Time:** ○○○○○

Forget about expensive games consoles – for hours of telly-free fun, all you really need is a piece of chalk!

There are many simple games you can play that are fun for all the family, adults as well as children. Here are a few to get you started:

Target
Players: 2 or more. Equipment: Chalk, pebble

Chalk an archery-style target on the ground with five rings, one inside the other. A couple of meters away, draw a straight line behind which throwers must stand.

Players then take turns to throw the pebble at the target, aiming for the middle. The inner circle scores 10 points, the next one 8, the next 6, the next 4, and the outside ring 2. If the pebble lands between two rings, the lower scoring one counts.

Players take turns and have five throws each. Whoever has most points after all have thrown is the winner.

Tic Tac Toe
Players: 2. Equipment: Chalk

This simple game for two players is also called Noughts and Crosses. Create a grid with nine squares by chalking two vertical lines across two horizontal ones.

The first player draws a cross in one box. Their opponent then draws a circle in another, and so on. The winner is the first to get a horizontal, vertical or diagonal line of three noughts or crosses.

Four By Four

Players: 2 (can also play as teams). Equipment: Chalk

This is a more challenging version of Tic Tac Toe. Start by chalking a 4 x 4 grid, which of course will have a total of 16 squares. Players take turns adding noughts or crosses as before, until all the boxes are filled.

The winner is the player who has the most lines of three, including horizontal, vertical and diagonal.

Human Snakes And Ladders

Players: 2 or more. Equipment: Chalk, dice

Draw a board with twenty squares, each large enough to stand on, in four rows of five. Number the squares from one at the bottom left to 20 at the top left, going left to right in the first row, right to left in the second, and so on. Between some numbers draw snakes, which cause the player to slide back. Between other numbers draw ladders, which help the player move closer to the finish. Use a die to determine how many squares you move. The first player to reach number 20 wins the game.

Tightrope

Players: 2 or more. Equipment: Chalk

Chalk a long line along the ground with some wiggles and bends in it. At a few points, leave a short break in the line as well.

The line is the tightrope. Players have to walk along it without stepping off at any point (if they do, they will fall and be eaten by crocodiles). When they come to the breaks, they must jump over them and land on the line where it starts again. Anyone falling off must start again at the beginning.

Chalk games are great fun on a sunny day!

#66 BECOME A KARAOKE STAR

Budget: $$$ **Time:** ◷◷◷◷◷

Karaoke gives everyone the chance to release their inner pop star!

In karaoke you sing along to recorded music using a microphone and a public address system. The music is usually a well-known pop song without the lead vocal. Lyrics are generally displayed on a video screen, together with a moving symbol, changing color, or music video images, to guide the singer.

If you live near any big city there are likely to be pubs, bars or clubs that offer karaoke at least once a week. Taking part is usually free, though you will of course need to buy a drink or two to warm up your vocal cords!

You can also get karaoke equipment for use at home. Nowadays this feature is increasingly included in home entertainment systems, or you can buy dedicated karaoke players fairly inexpensively. Note that you will also need to buy special disks of karaoke songs. Although some systems claim to let you use ordinary music CDs from which the vocals are filtered out, the results of this are generally disappointing.

Karaoke is great entertainment for a party, and of course anyone of any age can take part.

More Tips

• Breathe in deeply and fill your lungs.

• Don't be afraid of embarrassing yourself. The worst thing is to hold back.

• Pick a song you identify with – if you really 'feel' what you are singing, the emotion will come across in your voice.

• Hold the microphone at least six inches from your mouth, or you will end up sounding like Darth Vader.

• Sing loudly – your voice will sound best with some power behind it.

• Don't tap, drop or swing the microphone. Damaging the equipment will bring a rapid end to proceedings and could land you with a large bill.

• Never point the microphone at the loudspeaker, or you will get an ear-splitting feedback howl.

Karaoke Facts and Figures

• The word 'karaoke' comes from two Japanese words meaning 'empty' and 'orchestra'.

• There is no definitive list of top karaoke songs, but some all-time favorites include Dancing Queen and Waterloo by Abba, I Will Survive by Gloria Gaynor, I Did It My Way by Frank Sinatra, and Black Velvet by Alannah Myles.

• According to the website AskMen.com, the best song for men to sing is Steppenwolf's Born to be Wild.

• A popular game using karaoke is to type in a random number and call up a song, which participants then attempt to sing. This game has come to be called Kamikaze Karaoke or Karaoke Roulette.

• Throughout much of North America, live band karaoke is also popular. In this variation, singers perform to a live band instead of a pre-recorded backing track.

• Robbie Williams holds the record for the largest number of people singing karaoke at one time, for over 120,000 people singing 'Strong' live at Knebworth, England, in 2003.

Finally, remember that karaoke is meant to be fun. Applaud the other performers, however bad they are, and never make fun at anyone else's expense. Not everyone can be Michael Bublé or Celine Dion!

#67 TRY AN UNUSUAL SPORT

Budget: $$$ Time: 🕐🕐🕐🕐🕐

If you're bored with all the usual sports – or none of them appeal – why not try something a little bit different?

There are lots of possibilities to suit all ages and temperaments and fitness levels. Here are a few to set you thinking:

Dodgeball – As popularized by the 2004 Ben Stiller movie, this game has many variants, but classic dodgeball simply involves hitting people with a ball while avoiding getting hit yourself. It is usually played as a team sport. Once all the members of a team have been eliminated, the other team are declared the winners.

Croquet – This is a sport of strategy as well as skill. It involves hitting plastic or wooden balls with a mallet through hoops (also called 'wickets') embedded in a grass playing area. Garden croquet is easy to learn and great fun for friends and family on a sunny afternoon. Kits are available from toy stores and online, or you could even make your own.

Muggle Quidditch – Strange but true: the game for wizards and witches invented by J.K. Rowling now has a real-life equivalent open to anyone (though it is especially popular with students). It is played in mixed teams of seven, all of whom compete while riding broomsticks. There is now an International Quidditch Association and an annual Quidditch World Cup.

Chess Boxing – This fast-growing hybrid sport combines chess with boxing in alternating rounds. The sport was devised by French artist and filmmaker Enki Bilal in 1992, with the first real event taking place in 2003. The sport alternates between rounds of chess and boxing, until a checkmate or knockout decides the winner. A chess boxing match lasts up to eleven rounds, starting with a four-minute chess round and followed by two minutes of boxing.

Zorbing – This is the sport of rolling downhill inside an orb, generally made of transparent plastic. Zorbing is usually performed on a gentle slope, but can also be done on a level surface, allowing more rider control. Zorbers do not normally compete with one another. It will certainly get your adrenalin flowing, though!

Poohsticks – Finally, here's a nice, gentle sport for you. As described in The House at Pooh Corner by A. A. Milne, Poohsticks is a simple sport that may be played on any bridge over running water. Each player drops a stick on the upstream side of the bridge and the one whose stick first appears on the downstream side is the winner. The annual World Poohsticks Championships have been held at Day's Lock on the River Thames in the UK since 1984.

There are lots of other unusual sports too, so do a little research to see what's going on in your area, or just invite some friends over and start playing.

#68 MAKE YOUR OWN SOUP

Budget: $$$　　　　Time: 🕐🕐🕐🕐🕐

If we want soup nowadays most of us just reach for a tin, but it's very easy to make your own as well. Admittedly, it will take a bit longer, but it will be worth it!

Home-made soup is as fresh and healthy as it comes, without the preservatives and other chemicals in shop-bought soup. You can choose the exact ingredients to suit your taste. Making soup is also a great way to use up left-overs, and can save you a lot of money as well.

Here's a step-by-step guide you can use to make almost any soup:

Choose Your Fat
Your soup will (probably) need to start with some type of fat, such as olive oil or butter. This is to sauté vegetables such as onions and celery and help bring out their flavor.

Choose Your Base
The options here include chicken, beef or fish stock, tomato purée, and cream or milk. Pick one or two of these: stock mixed with tomato purée is delicious, for example, as is stock with milk. Choose the flavors you want from the ingredients you have available.

Choose Your Protein
This is optional, but if you want a source of protein in your soup, meat or fish are the main options. You could use chicken, ground beef, steak, or a flaky fish such as haddock. It's best to match this with your base for example beef and fish stock might not work so well.

Choose Your Vegetables
Onion is a common choice in soup because it imparts so much flavor. Garlic, carrots and celery are all popular too. Other possibilities include

beans, potatoes, spinach, kale, corn, peas and tomatoes.

Choose Your Spices

Salt and pepper are the two basic spices, so you will almost certainly want to include them. Here are a few other popular flavor combinations…

- Celery seed, marjoram, thyme, parsley and sage go well with chicken.
- Marjoram, rosemary and thyme can work well with beef.
- Basil, oregano or fennel go well with tomato-based soups.
- Chilis need chili powder and perhaps cumin.
- Cream soups can benefit from the addition of parsley or thyme.

There are many other possibilities as well, so experiment and see what you can come up with. Just remember to add a little at a time, and taste and adjust as you go.

Method

Having assembled your ingredients, here's how to cook them:

1. Heat a large soup pot over medium heat.
2. Sauté your aromatic vegetables (onion, garlic, celery, carrot) in your fat.
3. Pre-cook your protein if necessary (for example, stew beef).
4. Add your base (except milk or cream), vegetables, protein, and spices.
5. Taste and adjust.
6. Allow to simmer for an hour or two.
7. Taste and adjust again.
8. Add any cream or milk just before serving, and heat through

Using this method it's possible to make just about any soup with what you've got in your cupboards. Make note of successful combinations for next time too!

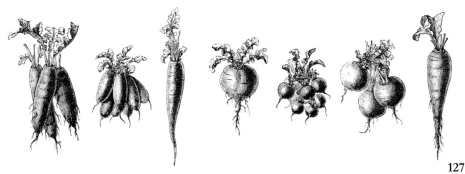

#69 MAKE YOUR OWN HERBAL TEA

Budget: $$$ Time: 🕐🕑🕒🕓🕔

Why pay through the nose for herbal tea from the shops, when it's so easy to make fresh at home? Teas made from fresh herbs are healthier and tastier, and in most cases you can grow them yourself as well!

Here are five herbs that make delicious teas and can be cultivated easily:

Camomile

Camomile tea is known for its soothing properties. It has small, feathery leaves and white, daisy-like flowers.

Growing: You can sow seeds in spring in a pot on your window-sill. Once germinated, plant them outside in a sunny, sheltered spot.

Preparation: Crop the chamomile when it is about 10 cm tall. Use a teaspoon of the flowers and leaves to make your tea, or dry the flowers and save them to use later. Infuse in hot water for around five minutes.

Fennel

This tall, willowy herb produces seeds with a distinctive anise favor. Fennel tea is said to have many health benefits, including anti-inflammatory properties and aiding digestion.

Growing: Fennel can be grown from seed or bought in garden centers. It grows quite high, so it's best to plant it at the back of a border in a sunny, well-drained position. Fennel goes to seed at the end of the summer, so let the seeds dry out on the plant and harvest them in the fall.

Preparation: Crush 1–2 teaspoons of seeds and infuse with boiling water.

Mint

Mint makes a zingy, refreshing tea. It's often taken after meals as an aid to digestion, and can also be used to treat an upset stomach. Spearmint and peppermint are the best varieties for making herbal tea.

Growing: Mint is a perennial plant. It can be grown more easily in a container, as it spreads easily and can choke off less vigorous plants around it. It dies off in the winter but starts to re-emerge in the spring.

Preparation: Pick sprigs of mint and infuse them for five minutes in boiling water.

Ginger

Ginger is a tropical, red-flowering plant, known for its ability to combat nausea.

Growing: Ginger can be grown indoors or outside in a warm, sheltered position. In the spring, plant a 'finger' of root ginger in a small pot. Keep it warm and moist on a sunny window-sill and transfer it to bigger pots as it grows. In the fall, let it dry out and lift out the roots.

Preparation: Place a slice of ginger root in a mug of boiling water and infuse for five minutes.

Bergamot

Bergamot is a member of the mint family, with leaves that have a delicate citrus flavor. It is said to have a range of health benefits, including lowering cholesterol.

Growing: Sow the seeds indoors in spring or outdoors after frost in pots. Thin out the seedlings and grow in full sun or partial shade, and avoid over-watering.

Preparation: Infuse 1/4 cup of the fresh leaves in boiling water for five minutes, and strain before drinking. You can also use the leaves to give black tea a delicious 'Earl Grey' flavor. Just add a tablespoon of bergamot leaves to the teapot and infuse for five minutes.

#70 PLAY A GAME OF FRISBEE

Budget: $$$ Time: 🕐🕐🕐🕐🕐

Everyone enjoys a game of Frisbee on a warm, sunny day. Round up a few friends and family (dogs love to play Frisbee too!) and head off to your nearest park or sports field. You'll have hours of fun, and some welcome fresh air and exercise too.

Some people find throwing a Frisbee challenging at first, so here's a guide to the classic backhand technique:

1. Grip the Frisbee in your fist. Your thumb should be on top of the Frisbee, your index finger should be against the edge, and your remaining fingers should touch the underside. The Frisbee should be held flat (horizontally) and not at an angle to the ground.

2. Stand with your feet at a 90-degree angle to your target (which will usually be another person). Your right foot should be in front if you are right-handed, and your left foot should be in front if you are left-handed.

3. Curl your wrist slightly back toward your body as you hold the Frisbee. Your elbow should be pointing up and outward.

4. Move your arm forward quickly. Straighten your arm and, as your arm is almost fully extended, flick your wrist and release the Frisbee with a spring-like motion toward your target. Aim to release the Frisbee just below your belly button, so it will fly in a straight line instead of up in the air.

When catching the Frisbee, clap your hands together just as it flies in between them. If you can see that it is too high for you to catch, move backward and jump at the appropriate moment to give yourself a few extra inches in height. It looks spectacular when it works!

#71 START A QUIZ TEAM

Budget: $$$ Time: 🕐🕐🕐🕐🕐

If you think your general knowledge is good, why not put it to the test and start a quiz team?

Quizzes are popular across the world. Typically they are held in pubs, bars and clubs. They are either one-off events with multiple teams competing, or two teams competing against each other in a weekly quiz league.

Quiz teams normally consist of four players, though the rules are often quite relaxed, and teams may have fewer or more players than this, up to a maximum set by the organizers.

A typical quiz has rounds on various subjects. Each round will have up to ten questions, and teams confer and write their answers on an answer sheet. As well as subjects such as history, geography and entertainment, there are often special rounds. These may include a music round, where teams have to identify a song or artist from listening to a snippet. There may also be a picture round, where teams have to identify celebrities, places or objects from images supplied on a photocopied sheet.

At the end of the quiz (or after each round) answers are handed in and scores worked out by the quizmaster, or teams may exchange and mark one another's answers. Usually a small prize is awarded to the winning team and maybe the runners-up.

If you want to start your own quiz team, you will need to do a little research to see what events take place in your area. In many cases all you will need to do then is turn up with your team on the night. Entry may be free or there may be a small charge to cover costs and perhaps provide prize money. If you want to join a quiz league you will need to find out who the organizers are and ask to register a team. You may have to wait until the start of a new season before you can start playing in the league.

#72 SET YOURSELF SOME GOALS

Budget: $$$ Time: 🕐🕐🕐🕐🕐

There's a great quote from Canadian academic and author Laurence J. Peter: 'If you don't know where you are going, you will probably end up somewhere else.'

Taken literally, of course, that's nonsense – if you don't know your destination, how can you wind up somewhere different? And yet this quote, tongue-in-cheek though it is, contains an important truth. If you have no goals and simply drift through life, it's unlikely you will achieve anything worthwhile.

So here's a little challenge for you – put down the TV remote and take control of your own life by setting yourself some goals or targets to achieve in the next twelve months.

Your goals might include anything from learning a new skill (there are lots of ideas elsewhere in this book), to getting a better job, meeting the love of your life, or setting up your own business. Other possible goals could include losing weight, giving up smoking, or taking more exercise.

To be fully effective, goals should be SMART. This is an acronym to help you remember the five principles of effective goal-setting. These are as follows…

S means Specific – Rather than 'I want to boost my income', a specific goal might be 'I want to be earning $1,000 a month more by this time next year'.

M means Measurable – This might be in financial terms, as in the last example, or simply in terms of numbers. For example, 'By the end of this month I will have submitted my résumé to fifty potential employers.'

A is short for Actionable – This means goals should be expressed in a way that can be put into action. A goal such as 'I want to be a successful author' is too vague to provide a useful target. A goal such as 'I will complete five short stories by the end of next month' is actionable, and therefore much more helpful.

R stands for Realistic – Goals should be challenging, of course, but they must also be realistic. If you set goals that are impossible to achieve, you will only become discouraged when you fail. It's better to set yourself more modest goals to start with, and make them more challenging if you find you are achieving them easily.

T stands for time-specific. Always set yourself deadlines for achieving any particular goal, and do your best to meet them. If you fail to do so, it's not the end of the world – but immediately set yourself another deadline (maybe a more realistic one) and do all you can to ensure that this time you succeed in meeting it.

Write down your goals and deadlines, and regularly monitor your progress toward achieving them. To accomplish your goals, of course, you will sometimes need to be flexible. You might need to take a break, for example, or adopt completely new tactics. But be prepared to try and try again to achieve your goals – and once you have done so, set yourself some new ones!

#73 READ A BOOK

Budget: $$$ Time: ①①①①①

In this fast-moving, pressurized world, isn't it time you rediscovered the simple pleasure of immersing yourself in a good book?

Whatever your interests, there's bound to be a book that appeals to you. If you enjoy nonfiction, you can take your pick from subjects including travel, history, humor, cooking, crafts and hobbies, biographies, self-help, science, nature, and many more.

Of course, if your tastes run to fiction, the choice is even larger. As well as classic and literary fiction, there are genres including romance, crime or detective, mystery, science fiction, fantasy, horror, historical, action or adventure, and so on, most with a variety of distinctive sub-genres as well.

With all this choice, how do you pick the right book for you? One solution is to ask friends and relatives with similar tastes for their recommendations. You can then have fun comparing your impressions of the book once you have read it.

In addition, many newspapers and magazines publish book reviews that can guide you, though always remember that these are only one person's opinion. You could also simply browse the bestsellers rack in your local bookstore or supermarket. Often, reading the blurb and maybe the first page or two will give you a good idea whether you will enjoy a book or not.

Another invaluable source of ideas for books to read is the internet. At the popular Amazon online store, you can browse many hundreds of titles in the category or genre of your choice. A further big attraction of Amazon (and similar sites) is that you can read reviews from other readers. Again, these shouldn't be taken as gospel, but reading a selection should help you decide whether this is the book for you.

There are also websites designed to help you discover books you might enjoy reading. One of the best known is Goodreads.com. On this site you can enter any titles or genres you've enjoyed in the past, and the site will recommend other books you might enjoy based on this. You can also become 'friends' with other members whose tastes are similar to yours, and see what they are currently reading.

Book or E-Book?

While print books are still popular, online at any rate e-book sales have overtaken them. You can read e-books on dedicated reading devices such as the Amazon Kindle, and also on tablets and smartphones with the aid of a suitable app.

E-books have some advantages over print books. One is that you can download them instantly from Amazon or another online store. You can have lots of e-books on the go at any one time if you like, all saved onto one lightweight device. And e-books are generally cheaper than print (though the saving isn't always as big as you might expect).

Of course, many people still prefer the look and feel of a 'real' book, and they are easier to lend to friends or simply donate after you have read them. The choice is yours, though. The likelihood is that while e-books will carry on growing in popularity, print books will still be around for a considerable time to come!

#74 LEARN TO PLAY THE GUITAR

Budget: $$$ Time: ○○○○○

Who doesn't love the idea of rocking out an arena on guitar, while an audience of adoring fans looks on? Unfortunately, as anyone who has ever tried will tell you, it's not as easy as top guitarists like Jimmy Page and Keith Richards make it look.

Still, with practice, anyone can learn to play a few songs on the guitar – and if you enjoy it and are willing to stick at it, there is nothing to stop you becoming the front man or woman of your own band!

Your first decision will be what type of guitar to start with. Most people choose an acoustic, but other options include electric guitar, bass guitar, tenor guitar, and classical or Spanish guitar (which is similar to an acoustic, but has nylon strings and a more mellow sound).

Once you've made your choice, your first step should be to learn the names and functions of the parts of your guitar, and how they work together. Learn how sound is emitted from the guitar, and how tension affects the strings. A little time spent developing this basic understanding will repay itself many times over in your learning and playing.

You can teach yourself the basics from books and websites, but sooner or later you're likely to need instruction from a guitar teacher. Most teachers come to students' own homes to teach, but some prefer to operate from their own home or studio. Lessons typically take an hour or so. Before signing up with a guitar teacher, check their qualifications and ask if you can speak to some of their current or former students.

<u>More Tips</u>

• Regular practice is key to learning to play the guitar. Aim to practice every day for at least half an hour.

• One thing all guitarists have to accept is that they will develop calluses (patches of hardened skin) on their fingers. This will be painful at first, but once you have developed them, the pain will disappear. The more you practice, the faster this will happen.

• Learn to read guitar music. The most popular system is called guitar tablature, or 'tab' for short. In tab each note is indicated by a number which indicates the fret to play, on the appropriate string. Most people find tab easier to follow than conventional sheet music (though it's worth learning that as well).

• Learn as many different ways to play a chord as you can. For instance, there are 10 different fret hand positions for playing the C chord. The more ways you know to play a chord, the more flexibility you'll have in moving from one to another.

• Play along with CD or MP3 versions of songs you like. Rewind and repeat any portions of a song you find difficult until you have mastered them.

• There are many websites that can help you learn (and improve) your guitar skills. For starters, try FretJam.com, Ultimate-Guitar.com and http://learnguitarfasttips.com. It's also well worth searching on YouTube for video guitar tutorials.

Finally, don't be too hard on yourself if you find guitar playing difficult at first. Just take your time and practice regularly. You'll get there in the end!

#75 JOIN A COMMUNITY THEATRE COMPANY

Budget: $$$ Time: ⏰⏰⏰⏰⏰

In most towns and cities there are community theatre companies, which are always looking for new members. In some countries (e.g. the United Kingdom) they are more commonly known as amateur theatre companies.

You don't have to be an aspiring actor to join a community theatre company. People are also needed for many other duties, including stage management, sound and lighting, costumes, front-of-house, publicity, props and stage design, and so on. Most people in community theatre aren't paid and do it for the love of it, although some view it as a stepping stone on the path to becoming a professional actor.

While some companies perform mainly traditional plays, from Shakespeare to Tennessee Williams, others specialize in musicals. As well as acting, performers in these shows are likely to be required to sing and dance as well.

Production standards in community theatre shows are typically high, often approaching professional level. Although most of the performers and backstage people do not receive any fees, audiences will still have to pay for tickets, so a good overall standard is essential.

Acting in Community Theatre

Most people join community theatre companies in the hope of getting an acting role. In order to act on stage, you will obviously need the confidence to perform to a live audience. That doesn't necessarily mean you must be an extrovert; some normally quiet people find that as long as they have a script to follow they can adopt any role. If the thought of performing to hundreds of people makes you very anxious, however, you might prefer to apply for backstage work initially.

Two skills you must have in order to act are the ability to project your voice to all parts of a venue, and the ability to learn lines. Some people are better at learning lines than others, but most find that they improve with practice.

Another aspect of community theatre to bear in mind is that it can be time-consuming. If you have a major role in a production, you may be expected to attend rehearsals three or more evenings a week for several months. You may then have to attend for technical rehearsals, dress rehearsals and the production run itself, which can be anything from one night to a week or longer.

Being involved in community theatre is a serious commitment, therefore, but it does offer many satisfactions and benefits too. Many find it a great way of making new friends; and the experience of working with a (possibly quite disparate) group of people to create a show audiences enjoy can be both fulfilling and addictive.

To find some community theatre companies near you, search online for "community theatre" or "amateur theatre" plus the name of your town or city.

Good luck, and see you on the stage!

#76 IMPROVE YOUR MEMORY

| Budget: $$$ | Time: ⏱⏱⏱⏱⏱ |

Many of us complain we have a 'memory like a sieve', as though there's nothing we can do about it. That's not the case, though.

Here are some easy techniques to help you remember basic (but important) information. Just taking a few minutes to learn and apply these methods really can make a big difference to your ability to memorize information.

How To Remember People's Names

Who hasn't suffered the embarrassment of being introduced to someone, only to discover later that they have already forgotten their name?

The ability to remember names is an invaluable skill in both social and business situations, so use this simple method to ensure you never forget one.

When introduced to somebody, try to create a mental image to help you remember their name. For example, you could visualize them standing beside someone you already know (a friend, maybe, or a celebrity) with the same or a similar name. When you see them again, this image will hopefully pop into your head and remind you of their name.

This 'association' method can be used in other ways too. For example, you could link their name to another word starting with the same letter or one that rhymes with it. If introduced to a Sandra, for example, you could associate her in your mind with a squirrel; if meeting a Jerry, associate him with a berry. Try to create vivid, unusual mental images to establish the link – for example, Jerry trying to eat a giant berry! Any time you see that person again, the mental image you created should help you recall their name.

Another good method is to choose a distinguishing feature about the person and link it with their name. If introduced to someone named Bill with tousled hair, for example, you might create a mental image of him paying a huge bill at the hairdresser's. Thankfully, you don't have to share your image with the person concerned!

How To Remember Pin Numbers

One unavoidable aspect of living in the 21st century is the need to remember PIN numbers for credit cards, websites, and so on. If you have trouble remembering these numbers, here's a simple method that can help. Start by memorizing the following list:

0 – toe	4 – door	8 – gate
1 – gun	5 – hive	9 - vine
2– shoe	6 – sticks	
3 – tree	7 – heaven	

As you'll see, each digit has a rhyming object associated with it. Now, say you have to remember the number 5376. Create a series of mental images using the relevant items from the list. So you might imagine a bee-hive (5) being pushed into the sky by a fast-growing tree (3), which keeps going up until it gets to heaven (7), where St Peter taps it with some sticks (6), and all the bees fly out and sting him!

Any time you need to remember the number in future, just replay this bizarre 'mind movie' in your head and you will have no problem recalling it.

These simple memory techniques can be adapted for many other situations as well. Why not start using them today, and leave any associations you might have with a sieve firmly in the kitchen!

#77 TRY CARVING FRUITS & VEGETABLES

Budget: $$$ Time: ◐◐◐◐◐

Fancy yourself as a sculptor, but put off by the difficulty (and cost) of carving stone? Then why not try fruit or vegetable carving instead? It's quick and easy to get started – and after all your friends and family have admired your masterpiece, you can eat it!

The tradition of food carving originated hundreds of years ago at Thai, Japanese and Chinese royal feasts, and it still features in restaurants serving oriental cuisine today. In recent times it has also become a big attraction on cruise liners, with passengers gathering in large numbers to watch demonstrations of the art by skilled chefs.

What You Will Need

To get started in fruit and vegetable carving all you really need are a small paring knife and a peeler, of the sort to be found in any kitchen.

Wooden toothpicks can be useful for assembling multi-part carvings. And another handy tool is a melon baller, which will let you create perfect spheres of melons, papayas, potatoes, radishes and other vegetables.

If you become really keen you can order specialty knife sets from websites such as Artchef.com. These include carving knives in a range of shapes and sizes, and other useful tools as well. The latter include so-called 'loop tools' for hollowing out, notching, marking and smoothing surfaces.

Whatever tools you use, the most important thing is that they are as sharp as possible. Not only will this give the best results, a sharp knife (properly used) is less likely to slip and injure you. A ceramic knife sharpener is another essential purchase for any serious fruit and vegetable carver.

What To Carve

You can carve almost any fruit or vegetable. One very popular choice, however, is watermelon. Not only are these large and relatively inexpensive, you can make good use of the contrast between the dark green skin, the pale green outer layer and the pink inner flesh.

Smaller fruit and vegetables can be transformed into flowers and leaves, as well as birds, fish, cats, frogs, butterflies, and even dragons. Skilled carvers can create anything from a delicate tomato rose to accompany a salad through to a stunning centerpiece to grace any banqueting table.

<u>More Tips</u>

• If you plan to eat your carvings, be sure to wash your hands before starting, and observe all the normal hygiene precautions.

• Use fresh fruit and vegetables at the stage just before they are ripe.

• Work as quickly as possible to keep your carving fresh.

• Carve gently, so that the fruit/vegetable does not break or bruise.

• Avoid carving out any more flesh than is necessary.

For more inspiration, see the Pinterest board by Maria del Pinto at http://tinyurl.com/vegcarving. The Templeofthai.com website also hosts a growing number of step-by-step tutorials, on subjects including radish flowers, carrot and cucumber leaves, yellow pumpkin roses, and a variety of beautiful watermelon carvings.

Have fun, and let your imagination run riot!

#78 PLAY A GAME OF CHARADES

Budget: $$$ Time: 🕐🕐🕐🕐🕐

In the days before TV, Charades was a popular parlor game, and it's still far more entertaining than most of what's on telly! The object of Charades is to communicate a word or phrase without using any spoken words.

Charades is a great party game, but you can also play it any time with friends or family. It's suitable for all ages, though aim to ensure that the answers will be familiar to everyone taking part. Once you've got your group together, here's a seven-step guide to playing Charades:

1. Cut out strips of paper and write different words or short phrases on each one. Good choices can include popular movies, TV shows, books or songs. Start with about five pieces of paper per player.

2. Fold all the slips of paper and put them in a box. The first player then picks one at random and opens it to reveal the contents without showing anyone else. He or she must then convey this non-verbally to the other players.

3. The player usually starts with a gesture to show the nature of their word or phrase. In classic Charades, the options are as follows:

Quotations: denoted by fingers of both hands making quote signs.
Movies: one hand held up to eye as if looking through a camera lens, one hand cranking like an old-fashioned movie camera.
Books: hands together in front of you, then opening out like a book.
Plays: down on one knee, arms out in a flamboyant 'acting' gesture.
Songs: hands moving out from mouth.
TV Shows: index fingers forming a small rectangle.

4. The player can then communicate how many words by raising that number of fingers – three fingers means three words, and so on. They may then raise one finger to indicate that they are about to convey the first word.

5. The player then acts out each word in turn, but without saying anything out loud. The other players guess, and when they get it right he rewards them with a thumbs-up or whatever.

6. Use nonverbal hints to indicate the type of word. Some common hints include 'sounds like', for which you would cup your hand to your ear, and 'short word', where you hold your thumb and index finger close together.

7. When someone guesses the entire phrase correctly, that's the end of the round. The person who guessed goes next, or you can take it in turns.

<u>More Tips</u>

• Charades is also a great team game. In this case divide everyone into two teams. Each team then writes words and phrases for their opponents, so you will need two boxes for players to pick from. Teams play alternately, and each correct guess scores one point.

• You may want to set a time limit for players to guess correctly, especially if you are playing in teams.

• If you have problems coming up with suitable terms for guessing, websites provide suggestions. Try PlayCharades.net or Charades-ideas.com.

#79 GO BOWLING

Budget: $$$ Time: 🕐🕐🕐🕐🕐

A trip to a bowling alley is fun for all ages, and can be surprisingly inexpensive too. You can also get combined or party tickets, which entitle you to a meal and drinks as well as use of the lane for a set time and/or number of games.

1. Bowling Basics

Bowling is played in lanes that are 60 feet long from the foul line to the head pin. There are gutters either side of the lane and if a ball falls into these it is out of play and doesn't score. A bowler must not overstep the foul line during his approach, or his shot won't count.

Ten pins are placed at the end of the bowling lane at the start of every frame. They are set out in four rows in a triangle formation, with the point facing the bowler. All pins earn the bowler one point each if they are knocked over.

2. Rules and Scoring

A bowling game consists of 10 frames. Each frame is equal to one turn for the bowler.

The bowler's objective is to knock over as many pins as possible in a frame, ideally all ten. A bowler can roll the ball twice per frame, provided he does not hit a strike (all pins down in the first throw). In that case his turn is over.

If a bowler still has some pins standing after his second throw (known as an open frame), he simply gets a point for each one he hit. If he gets a strike (all knocked down by the first throw) or a spare (all knocked down after two) the scoring is a bit more complicated.

If a bowler gets a spare, after his next turn he receives 10 points plus the number of pins he knocks down with the first roll of his next turn. So if he then knocks down 3 pins, then he will get a total of 13 points for the frame in which he got a spare.

If a bowler gets a strike, he earns ten points plus the number of pins knocked over on his next two throws. If he gets two more strikes, for example, his total score for the first one will be 10 + 10 + 10 = 30 points. The most a bowler can score in one game is 300 points (30 x 10). The winner of the game is the player with most points after everyone has bowled 10 frames.

In practice, most bowling alleys have automated scoring systems, but these can sometimes malfunction, so it is just as well to understand the scoring yourself.
Bowling is great fun, and if you get the bug you may want to buy your own bowling shoes and balls rather than hiring them from the alley, and maybe even join a bowling club.
Even if you don't want to take it that far, though, a trip to a bowling alley is still a hugely enjoyable way to spend a few hours in the company of friends or family!

#80 VISIT AN AMUSEMENT PARK

Budget: $$$ Time: 🕐🕐🕐🕐🕐

A trip to an amusement park makes a great day out, and it needn't break the bank either. Family tickets can be great value if going with children, and there are often discounts and special offers as well. Check on the park's website beforehand to see if there are any deals you can take advantage of.

Most people are familiar with the Disney parks, but there are many lesser-known but still very entertaining parks in every corner of the globe. Here is a small selection that offer great rides, beautifully themed areas, relaxing gardens, and more…

Europa Park, Rust, Germany: The theme of this park is Europe itself, with thirteen different areas each showcasing a particular country. The food and rides are both top quality.

Knoebel's Amusement Resort, Elysburg, Pennsylvania, USA: This old-time-themed rural park features excellent roller-coasters, one of the world's best dark rides, and one of the few carousels where you can still grab for the brass ring.

Tivoli Gardens, Copenhagen, Denmark: Rides, fine-dining restaurants and a magical atmosphere combine in this park at the center of Copenhagen. The old-time funhouse and brakeman-driven scenic railway are two of its top attractions.

Pleasure Beach, Blackpool, England: This popular non-themed park has a mixture of old-time and modern rides. They include four wooden roller-coasters and one of the world's few Derby Racers (an intense, carousel-like ride).

Holiday World, Santa Claus, Indiana, USA: This holiday-themed park has three top-rated wooden roller-coasters, including The Voyage, considered by many the world's best wooden coaster. Santa is in residence all the year round.

Tripsdrill, Cleebronn, Germany: Clever theming, fun rides and little surprises are the rule here, from the Bathtub Flume to the Vinarium (wine museum). Tripsdrill boasts over 100 original attractions, nestled amid flourishing natural surroundings.

Dreamworld, Coomera, Gold Coast, Australia: Dreamworld is Australia's biggest theme park. It is split into loosely themed zones, including Main Street, Town of Gold Rush, and Rocky Hollow. The two biggest attractions are the Tower of Terror and Giant Drop.

More Tips

• Aim to arrive early, ideally half an hour before the park opens. That way you'll be ahead of the crowd and be able to enjoy at least two or three major rides with little to no wait.

• If there's a major new attraction everyone wants to try, either go there first or leave it till late in the day, when many people are heading home and queues get shorter.

• Bring your own food and drink, as food at amusement parks is often over-priced and may be poor quality (though in recent years the food on offer at many parks has improved considerably).

• Take a cagoule or waterproof poncho for protection on the water rides (or if it rains).

• Especially if with young children, schedule regular breaks for relaxing. Spending the whole day rushing from one ride to the next is exhausting and most likely to end in tears.

Have a great time, and start planning your next amusement park trip as soon as you get back!

#81 SERVE ENGLISH AFTERNOON TEA

Budget: $$$ Time: ◷◔◷◷◷

Afternoon tea is a fine English tradition. You can enjoy it in hotels in Britain and many other parts of the world, but why not prepare it yourself, and invite all your friends round for a wonderfully civilized afternoon tea party?

Ideally, to serve afternoon tea you should have a tiered cake stand. The idea is that each level is used for something different: typically sandwiches at the bottom, cakes in the middle, and scones or petits fours at the top.

If you don't have a cake-stand, you may be able to pick one up cheaply from a local thrift store. Otherwise, use your best crockery and make it more special with lace doilies, folded napkins, and so on. You will also need a teapot, tea-strainer, teacups, cutlery, and cake-slices for serving.

The Food

There are no strict rules when it comes to food, but a standard afternoon tea would include a selection of sandwiches, cakes, and scones or teacakes.

Sandwiches are easy to make. It's good to use both white and brown (wholemeal) bread. Popular fillings include salmon and cucumber, cheese and pickle, ham, egg and cress, prawn mayonnaise, and roast chicken or beef. You might also want to prepare some vegetarian sandwiches (cucumber is very traditional, and fresh tomato with basil and a vinaigrette dressing is delicious).

Whatever fillings you choose, make your sandwiches small and dainty, and cut off the crusts: you don't want your guests filling up on bread so they have no room for anything else!

Scones can be bought from the shops, but they will be much fresher and tastier if you bake them yourself. The BBC Good Food website has an excellent recipe at http://tinyurl.com/sconerecipe, which you can prepare and cook in twenty minutes. Scones are traditionally served with jam and clotted cream. Again, you can use shop-bought jam if you like, or (much better) serve your own home-made version.

Other foods you could offer include buns, teacakes, crumpets, muffins, eclairs, macaroons, biscuits (cookies), cakes, and so on. Serve them all in small, finger-food portions.

The Drinks

Tea is, of course, the one essential component of English afternoon tea. Be sure to make it in a pot with loose tea rather than tea-bags!

Ensure that milk and sugar are on the table (in dainty jugs and serving bowls) for guests to add according to their taste. For a larger party you could offer a choice of teas, perhaps including Earl Grey, Darjeeling, peppermint, chamomile and, of course, the traditional English Breakfast. In hot weather you could offer iced tea as a cooling alternative.

Of course, if you really enjoy English afternoon tea, there is no reason you couldn't just make it for you and your partner, or even just yourself. Sip your tea, eat a cucumber sandwich, then close your eyes and imagine yourself on an English village green watching a game of cricket!

#82 ATTEND A FESTIVAL

Budget: $$$ **Time: ① ① ① ① ①**

Instead of watching your favorite stars on TV, why not go to a festival and see them performing live?

In recent years the number of festivals has mushroomed, and for many people going to one has become an essential part of their summer. Music festivals are obviously the most popular, but there are also dance festivals, drama festivals, film festivals, ethnic arts festivals, book festivals, and more. Large festivals such as SXSW (South by South West) in Austin, Texas and Glastonbury in England often feature a variety of art forms as well as music.

Some festivals require a ticket. Although tickets for the big festivals can be pricy, it is a still a lot cheaper than buying concert tickets for all the bands, and you get the whole festival experience thrown in as well. Smaller festivals are generally cheaper, and there are also free festivals sponsored by local government, city councils, community groups, and so on. Most people going to a festival take tents and camp on the site, though smaller local festivals may attract mainly day visitors.

There are various resources you can use to find out about forthcoming festivals. Newspapers, the music press and listings magazines normally carry adverts and often editorial coverage for the main festivals. There are also websites such as MusicFestivalJunkies.com and JamBase.com/festivals that list a wide range of forthcoming events. Finally, you could simply search Google for 'Festival' along with the name of your city, state or area. Going to a festival can be hugely enjoyable, but it's important to take a few basic precautions to avoid any problems.

<u>More Tips</u>

• Only pack what you can carry. Car parks and camp sites can be a long way apart, and you don't want to spend half a day going back and forth carrying things around. You can always pick up any bits and pieces you need from the site shops (though they may cost a bit more).

• Don't be tempted to bring expensive, valuable items such as jewelry or a brand new iPod to a festival – the risk of losing them or having them damaged or stolen is just too great.

• Take enough cash with you to at least cover the essentials. Most sites have cash machines, but they are likely to have long queues. Keep your money in various pockets or places in your bag to reduce the impact if any is lost or stolen.

• Find a good spot to pitch your tent, not too close to the action (more risk of intruders) but not too far away either. It's also good to get to know your neighbors, so you can agree to keep an eye on one another's stuff.

• Take precautions to guard against the sun. That means using plenty of sunblock, and maybe wearing a hat and sunglasses as well.

Have a great time, and enjoy all the fun of the festival!

#83 GROW YOUR OWN STRAWBERRIES

Budget: $$$ Time: 🕐🕐🕐🕐🕐

Strawberries are delicious to eat and easy to cultivate. You can grow them almost anywhere: your garden, a container, a hanging basket, or even your windowsill. Strawberries are therefore suitable for even the most space-limited gardeners!

There are various types of strawberry you can grow, according to your tastes and the room you have available. The most popular are ever-bearing or perpetual strawberries. These produce a steady supply of fruit throughout the year.

Other options include summer-fruiting strawberries, which produce one large crop in early to mid-summer (good for jam-makers), and alpine strawberries. The latter are smaller, more delicate-looking plants, which produce large numbers of small fruits that are crammed with flavor.

Growing in the Garden

The easiest way to get started with strawberries is to buy small plants from garden centers. The best time to plant will depend on the variety you've chosen, so read the label or ask someone at the garden center for advice.

Choose a warm and sunny spot in your garden. Strawberries do best in direct sunlight, and they also appreciate minimal wind.

Dig over the soil well, removing any weeds and roots, and add well-rotted organic compost to enrich it. It's also a good idea to apply a layer of mulch to protect the soil and keep the strawberries clean. Traditionally straw was used for this – hence the name, of course.

Plant the strawberries at least 12 inches apart, being sure to keep the crown (from which the stems emerge) above the soil line. Water regularly, but don't overdo it – strawberry plants have shallow roots that can easily dry out, but they don't like being soggy.

Pluck off the first flowers that appear, as this will encourage the plants to develop a stronger root system. It's also best to remove any runners, as these can deplete the energy of the plant and reduce the amount of fruit it produces.

Once the strawberries have turned from green to red it's time to pick them. Cut them off at the stalk, and give them a quick wash in cold water before eating them.

Growing in a Container

Strawberries are also easy to grow in pots and containers. You can place them on a balcony, patio or indoors in front of a sunny window.

Use a container with good drainage – placing small stones or fragments in the base will help – and two-thirds fill with potting compost. Give the soil a thorough watering, then place your strawberry plants in the pot with roots well spread and cover with more compost to the level of the crown. Water again, adding more soil if required, then put the containers in a sunny spot inside or out.

Enjoy your strawberries fresh with cream, in recipes, or make jam from them. You can also freeze them to enjoy in the winter. Not only are they full of flavor, they are low in calories and packed with vitamins and other nutrients, so you can eat as many as you like (within reason) with a clear conscience!

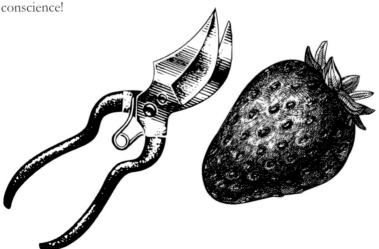

#84 HAVE A
PICNIC

Budget: $$$ Time: 🕐🕐🕐🕐🕐

Who doesn't enjoy a picnic on a warm, sunny day? You could just take your family, or invite all your friends as well.

Parks make great venues for picnics, with the advantage that there's likely to be car parking nearby, along with toilets and somewhere to shelter if the worst comes to the worst and it rains. But there are also designated picnic spots in many beautiful parts of the countryside, so do a little research to find out where would suit you best. Or, of course, you could simply have a picnic in your own back garden!

The most important thing you will need for your picnic is, of course, the food and drink. What you take is up to you, but be sure it's easy to transport and to eat. Some good food choices for picnics include:

• Sandwiches and bread rolls
• Wraps with salad
• Quiche and pizza slices
• Sausage rolls
• Asian snacks (e.g. bhajis, samosas and pakoras)
• Potato chips/crisps
• Pasta salad
• Sliced vegetables such as carrots and celery, and dips
• Fruits such as apples, bananas and watermelons

Avoid ice cream, sticky puddings, and cakes – they are fragile to transport, and will attract wasps and other insects. Drinks are important too: bring a choice, including bottled water, squash or fruit juice, and perhaps a flask of tea or coffee as well.

Pack the food in an insulated cool bag. Take disposable paper or plastic cups and plates. These are light to carry and will reduce the amount of washing-up when you get home.

Take a picnic blanket and (preferably) a waterproof groundsheet, especially if there has been rain recently, and set out your picnic on this. You might also want to bring fold-up chairs for older members of the party in particular.

More Tips

• Bring a ball or (even better) a Frisbee. This will give everyone a chance to stretch their legs and run off any surplus energy!

• Have a 'worst case scenario' plan in case the weather deteriorates, e.g. retiring to a nearby café or coffee shop.

• Take sensible precautions against the sun, including sunglasses and sun block, and perhaps a hat as well. This is particularly important for children, who will happily run around in the sun all day.

• Have some napkins or wet wipes available – bugs love sticky fingers.

• Be sure to clean up after you and remove any rubbish. It's a good idea to bring a large plastic bag for this purpose.

#85 TRY YOUR HAND AT COMPING

Budget: $$$ Time: 🕐🕐🕐🕐🕐

Comping is the name sometimes used to describe the hobby of entering consumer competitions and sweepstakes.

Some people are very successful at this, collecting a steady stream of prizes. These can include cash, cars, other valuable products, and luxury vacations.

Most competitions are run by companies to publicize their products. Entry forms are typically available from shops, magazines, newspapers, product packaging, and so on, and mailed in. A growing number, however, are run on the internet.

The type of competition most favored by serious compers requires entrants to produce as part of their entry a tie-breaker slogan. Typically they are asked to complete a sentence describing the sponsor's product in a way that is apt and original, or amusing. For example, when the jam-makers Robertsons asked contestants to suggest an ending for, 'A day begun with Robertsons' Shred', the winning entry was, '...would Rip Van Winkle out of bed!'

The big attraction of this sort of contest is that you really can use skill to give your chances a boost. It's a skill almost anyone can acquire with practice, and once you have done so, your entries will regularly find their way on to the judges' shortlists, and hopefully more.

Unfortunately this type of contest is not as common as it once was (though they can still be found). The majority nowadays require the completion of a simple task such as answering an easy question, or they are just prize draws or sweepstakes, where the winner/s are selected at random.
Clearly, there is less chance to use skill to improve your chances of winning these competitions, but it is equally true that somebody has to!

Some contests, especially those run online, allow multiple entries, so you can boost your chances by entering as often as the rules allow.

More Tips

• Look out for competitions run by local stores and other businesses, as these usually attract far fewer entries than national and web-based promotions.

• Read the rules carefully and follow them to the letter. In many contests a high proportion of entrants are eliminated because they failed to do this.

• Keep a record of what competitions you have entered and when. This is especially important with contests allowing multiple entries. You don't want to disqualify yourself by accidentally entering too often.

• Use colorful cards in mail-ins. There is evidence that such cards can boost your chances of success, as they stand out better in a large mass of entries.

• Make good use of the free websites aimed at competition enthusiasts. The ContestGirl.com site lists hundreds of contests and sweepstakes in the US and Canada, while for those in the UK and Ireland, ThePrizeFinder.com is an invaluable source of information.

Be patient and persistent when entering competitions. Even if you follow all the advice above, you won't win every time or anything like it. But remember too – every time you enter, the chances you will win a prize improve. In the words of the popular saying, 'You've got to be in it to win it!'

#86 PERFORM RANDOM ACTS OF KINDNESS

Budget: $$$ Time: 🕐🕐🕐🕐🕐

The idea of random acts of kindness (**RAKs** for short) may have come from the author Anne Herbert, who says she wrote 'Practice random kindness and senseless acts of beauty' on a place-mat at a Sausalito restaurant in the early 1980s. Another story credits the phrase to Bakersfield College professor Chuck Wall of Bakersfield, California.

Either way, a random act of kindness is a selfless act performed by a person (or persons) wishing to assist or cheers people up. Not only does performing RAKs help the recipients, it will make you feel better about yourself, and make the world a nicer and happier place all round!

The concept of random acts of kindness has been widely adopted, and there are various organizations and websites devoted to promoting it (e.g. RandomActsOfKindness.org). If you want to try it out yourself, here are some suggestions to get you started…

Ideas for RAKs

• Send a note of appreciation to someone who has been a good friend to you.

• When in line at a coffee or snack bar, randomly pay for your own order and that of someone behind you, expecting nothing in return.

• Reach out to someone you haven't spoken to for a while. Write them a letter or – even better – phone them up.

• Pay someone a compliment. It only takes a moment, and will brighten anyone's day.

• Have a clear-out and donate anything you no longer need to a charity or thrift shop, or offer it to a friend or neighbor.

• Write a thank-you letter to a business from which you have received good service. If you dealt with someone who was particularly helpful, be sure to mention them by name.

• Bake a cake for someone you know who has been going through a tough time and needs cheering up.

• Invite your neighbors over for afternoon tea or morning coffee.

• Send a friend a bunch of flowers to brighten their day and show you appreciate them.

• Clear litter and weeds from the street outside.

• Put a few coins or a note in an envelope and put it through a stranger's letterbox. On it write, 'Random acts of kindness – have a drink and a treat on me.'

• Take a housebound or elderly neighbor out for the day, or offer to do their shopping.

• If you see someone searching for change at a parking meter or supermarket checkout, give them the necessary coins yourself.

• Offer to babysit free of charge, so that the parents can have a night out together.

If you want more ideas take a look at the RandomActsOfKindness.org website mentioned earlier, which has hundreds of suggestions.

See also SocialStorehouse.com, which describes itself as the Random Acts of Kindness Network. Here people can request RAKs or donate them. The most asked-for items include blankets and bedding, coats, gloves, hats, backpacks, baby clothes, toys, gift cards, and cellphone credit.

Many people find that performing random acts of kindness is both fun and fulfilling, and they aim to ensure they complete at least one such act every day. Why not try it yourself, and see how it can change your own life for the better!

#87 JOIN AN EXERCISE CLASS

Budget: $$$ Time: 🕐🕐🕐🕐🕐

Nobody ever got any fitter watching TV, so why not do your body a favor and sign up to an exercise class?

As well as gyms and sports clubs, group exercise classes are held in schools and colleges, universities, community centers, and at nonprofit organizations such as the YMCA. You will normally have to pay a fee but these are generally quite reasonable. Discounts may be available for students, the unemployed, senior citizens, and so on.

There are lots of different types of exercise you could choose. A few possibilities are listed below.

Yoga – As well as doing wonders for your flexibility and posture, this age-old art can also significantly reduce your anxiety level and improve your mood. It's suitable for all ages and levels of athleticism.

Zumba – This dance-based program has become hugely popular in recent years. The exercises include music with fast and slow rhythms, as well as resistance training. The benefits include building strength and improving flexibility and posture. Zumba is a 'feel-happy' workout that is good for both the body and the mind.

Pilates – Pilates has some similarities with yoga, but it has a particular focus on strengthening your back and core. It is particularly good for firming your abdominal muscles. For general posture and flexibility, however, yoga may be preferable.

Spinning – This involves working out on stationary bikes, often mixing short, intense speed intervals and simulated hill climbs with periods at a regular, comfortable pace. It's great for losing weight and strengthening your heart.

Tai Chi – Tai Chi combines deep breathing and relaxation with slow and gentle movements. It can help reduce stress, improve balance and general mobility, and increase muscle strength in the legs. Tai Chi is a popular form of exercise among older people, although anyone can benefit from it.

More Tips

• Before signing up for any exercise class, ask if you can at least look in on a session to get an idea what to expect. Some organizers allow people to try a session for free to see if it will appeal to them or not.

• Speak to the class leader and ask about his/her qualifications to teach the exercise in question. Explain your own aims and general fitness level, and ask if you think the class would be suitable for you, or if there is another one they would recommend.

• Ask also about the preferred kit. Not only will this prevent you standing out unduly at the first session, having the right clothing and footwear will ensure you get the most from the exercise.

• Don't just stick to one class. Be open to trying different types of exercise, even if you're not sure you would like them. You may surprise yourself!

• Shop around to save money. Discount sites such as Groupon.com often offer cut-price deals on gym membership, exercise classes, and so on. Make good use of free-trial offers, and don't commit yourself to a package until you are sure you can (and will) make it to every class.

#88 VISIT A ZOO OR WILDLIFE PARK

Budget: $$$ Time: ◐◐◐◐◐

Who didn't enjoy a trip to the zoo as a kid? But even for adults, a visit can be an enjoyable and educational experience, and won't cost a fortune either.

Zoos offer the chance to view animals from across the world and learn more about them. In addition, many are heavily involved in conservation projects, where they care for endangered species, breed them, and ultimately return some to the wild. The thought may not be uppermost in your mind when planning a day out, but by visiting a zoo you are helping support this important work.

Most people have a zoo or wildlife park somewhere nearby. If you're not sure what there is, a quick search on Google for 'Zoo' plus the name of your city, state or region should turn up some possibilities. Most zoos have their own websites, so you can use these to check out the facilities and attractions on offer, plus entrance fees, travel directions, car parking, discounts, special events, and other useful information.

More Tips

• Most animals are more active in the mornings. Get there early and you'll beat the crowds and get the best show.

• Feeding time is always a popular attraction. Information is usually displayed prominently somewhere need the entrance, or ask a member of staff.

• Many zoos offer free talks and demonstrations during the day, and even guided tours. Again, check when you arrive, and incorporate any that sound interesting into your schedule.

• Don't try to do much, particularly if with children. Keep the pace relaxed, and incorporate regular breaks for refreshments or just sitting quietly watching the animals.

• Be safety aware. Don't allow children to breach the barriers or put their hands into cages or enclosures.

• Respect the animals, and encourage children to do likewise. Don't tap on the glass or otherwise tease them. Not only does this cause the animals stress, it could lead to accidents.

• If there is a petting zoo where children can touch the animals, ensure they wash their hands thoroughly afterwards. Don't allow children to take bottles, pacifiers or other items into the animal-contact area.

• Some zoos now have evening or late-night openings. This can be a great way to appreciate nocturnal species in particular, and the atmosphere can be more laid-back. Just be aware that many animals will be sleeping or preparing to sleep, so avoid making loud noises or otherwise disturbing them.

Finally, if there is a zoo or wildlife park near you that you plan to visit regularly, it's worth checking whether they have a membership scheme. Many do this in order to attract repeat visitors. You can save a lot of money compared with paying standard admission fees each time, and you may also get bonuses and other privileges. The zoo website should have information about this, or give them a call and ask.

165

#89 THROW A DINNER PARTY

Budget: $$$ Time: ⏰⏰⏰⏰⏰

Dinner parties aren't just for characters on Mad Men. They can be a great way to enjoy quality time with your friends and family, and you'll have the added satisfaction of providing a wonderful night's entertainment for them as well.

The number one secret to running a successful dinner party is planning. Choose guests who get on well and have at least some common interests. If you plan to shake things up by inviting someone nobody else knows, make sure they'll fit in and won't make the rest of your guests feel uncomfortable.

Plan your menu carefully in advance. A dinner party is not an occasion for wild experimentation, so choose dishes you have made successfully at least once or twice before.

It's also best to pick dishes you can prepare at least partly in advance. You want to avoid the scenario where everything has to be done at the last minute, so you're confined to the kitchen while all your other guests are enjoying themselves in the dining room.

Doing as much in advance as you can will help ensure you don't get stressed out on the night, and can relax and enjoy your guests' company.

More Tips

• Remember to ask in advance about any food allergies, special diets, or other preferences. Make at least two of your courses suitable for everyone, to save yourself work.

• Set the table in advance, with a tablecloth, napkins, wine glasses, cutlery, and so on, and a vase of flowers in the middle. Candles can provide a pleasant, restaurant-like ambience.

• Aim to include at least some seasonal food. Not only will it taste good, you'll get points for being in tune with the seasons too.

• Try to balance your menu – avoid having pastry or cheese in every course, for example. It can be a good idea to have a theme for the whole meal, e.g. Spanish, Italian or Mexican.

• Don't go overboard with the hors d'oeuvres. You don't want your guests to fill up on little snacks so they can't manage the main course you have labored long and hard over.

• Use finishing touches to give your presentation restaurant quality. A handful of rocket leaves or sprig of fresh herbs can be all it takes.

• Similarly, try to avoid serving food that is all the same color. Lift a lemon tart out of the ordinary with a sprinkling of raspberries or sprig of redcurrants, for example.

• Put on some unobtrusive background music to create the right atmosphere. Create a playlist in advance, or save yourself some time and let Pandora, Spotify, or Sirius radio do the job.

• Don't make the common mistake of neglecting the dessert. The evening should finish on a high note, not a let-down. Choose something light but delicious, and make an extra effort to ensure it impresses, both in appearance and flavor.

Finally, don't take your dinner party too seriously and stress out over any mistakes. The chances are your guests will be far too busy enjoying the food, drink and conversation to even notice. Relax, accept the compliments, and hope that someone else volunteers to tackle the washing up!

#90 GO GEOCACHING

Budget: $$$　　　Time: ○○○○○

Geocaching is an exciting, family-friendly pastime that will exercise both your mind and body. It is a sort of high-tech treasure hunt, where you use a GPS receiver to hunt for a cache of goodies hidden somewhere above ground.

Caches are placed all over the world by fellow geocachers, who assemble a collection of trinkets, a logbook and pen, and perhaps a disposable camera. This is then placed in a weatherproof box and hidden under a rock, behind a tree, or maybe even in a more urban locale.

The geographical coordinates of these containers are then posted on one of several websites for other geocachers to seek out. Once you have found a cache, you can help yourself to a trinket from it and replace it with one of your own.

Here is a quick step-by-step guide to starting out in geocaching:

1. You will need a portable GPS receiver or a smartphone with GPS capability. If you don't have one already, you may be able to borrow or hire one.

2. Create an account with a cache-listing website. Some are free, while others charge a modest fee to access certain features. Try a range of sites to see which you prefer. The biggest and best known is GeoCaching.com, but others include Navicache.com and http://brillig.com/geocaching/.

3. Search the site for caches hidden near you. There are literally millions of geocaches worldwide, so there are almost certain to be some in your area.

4. Pick a cache you like the sound of and note down any hints or clues.

Check the difficulty level as well (a five-star system is often used to rate this). You may not want to search for a cache that's too hard if you are just starting out.

5. Use the GPS unit to navigate your way to the cache: it should take you to within a few meters of the hiding place. After that you'll have to rely on your initiative, and any clues you may have been given.

6. Once you have found the cache, remember how it was concealed. You should leave everything just as you found it.

7. Browse the trinkets and take any one you wish, replacing it with something else of equal or greater value. You should also make an entry in the log-book, noting the date and your caching site user name.

8. Close the cache securely and leave it as you found it. When you get home, record your visit on your chosen caching website.

Just remember to stay safe and avoid going on private land without permission (caches are always hidden in publicly accessible places). Geocachers are also expected to leave the cache and surrounding area in as good a state (or better) as when they found it.

#91 LEARN TO SURF

Budget: $$$ Time: 🕐🕐🕐🕐🕐

Surfing, is a great form of exercise, and tremendous fun too. Admittedly, it's not easy at first, but the more you practice, the faster you will improve!

Obviously to surf you will need to be by the sea, but you can always learn the basics on vacation. Many people start by doing this, and then when they get hooked arrange regular trips to the coast, or even end up moving there!

Equipment

The most important thing you will need is, of course, a surfboard. There are various types, but as a beginner it's best to go for a larger board rather than a short one. Most people start with a longboard, the oldest and longest type of board, ranging from 8 to 12 feet in length.

If the sea is cold you will also need a wetsuit. This will keep your body warm in cold water, helping you avoid chills and hypothermia. The local surf shop will be able to advise you whether a wetsuit is needed or not.

Another thing you'll need is a leash to ensure you don't get separated from your board when you wipe out (fall off). And finally, you'll need some surfboard wax. This is an important and inexpensive product you can rub onto the top of a board to increase its grip, thus allowing better balance in the water.

If you're not sure whether surfing is for you, you can always hire the necessary equipment from the surf shop. You can also buy boards and other equipment second-hand. Surfing definitely doesn't have to be expensive!

Taking Lessons

Initially at least it's best to take lessons from a qualified surfing instructor. Not only will this build your confidence, the instructor will show you the proper techniques and ensure you stay safe.

If possible, try to book a place on a group class. It's much more fun learning with other beginners. You can help and encourage one another, and it can be reassuring to see that other people find it challenging as well!

The best place to ask about lessons is the surf shop. They may well offer tuition themselves, but if not they will be able to recommend instructors. You can also ask around local surfers. Most are very friendly, and happy to help novices.

More Tips

• Don't surf alone, especially as a beginner. Even having a friend on the shore is safer than going solo.

• Stay close to the beach, in surf that's suitable for beginners, until you're thoroughly experienced.

• If you feel you're about to wipe out, jump off to the side rather than in front or behind. Most surfing injuries are caused by collisions with the board.

• When you are surfing look the way you want to go (toward the shore) and not down at your board.

• Wear sunblock. The sun can be very strong on the sea, so it's important to protect exposed skin.

Most of all, though, relax and have fun. Surfers are friendly, sociable people who enjoy life to the full. If you go in with the same attitude, you will quickly be accepted as one of them.

#92 CREATE A ROCK GARDEN

Budget: $$$ Time: 🕐🕐🕐🕐🕐

A rock garden – or rockery if you prefer – makes a delightful addition to even the smallest garden. What's more, it's an easy project for even the most reluctant gardener to tackle, as well as being something the whole family can get involved with.

Start by identifying a suitable piece of ground and prepare it. An area that gets lots of sunshine is best. Dig out the soil to a depth of at least a foot, removing any weeds and roots. To improve drainage add a base layer of stones, broken bricks and clay pot fragments. Add a layer of coarse sand over this, and cover with six to nine inches of garden soil.

Now you can add the rocks. Ideally use rocks found naturally on your land, but if you don't have these you can get landscaping rocks from a garden center or home improvement store. Arrange them in a natural-looking way, ensuring that larger rocks are at least a third buried.

Add a layer of planting compost on top of the soil. Use a good multi-purpose compost mixed in equal parts with sharp sand or grit – again, this will help ensure good drainage.

You're now ready to add your plants (see below). Loosen their roots and plant them level with the surface, firming them gently in. Add more compost on top if required, and finish by applying a layer of grit or gravel to retain moisture and suppress weed growth. Water the plants in well, and continue to water regularly until they are established.

Choosing Your Plants

Most rock garden plants are small and compact, and tend to be tough and drought-resistant. Many flower profusely, in a range of brilliant colors. Your choice will depend to some extent on where you live. Alpines are a popular choice in temperate climates, while succulent plants and even cacti work well in hotter, drier climates.

Begin by planting a variety of species. As they grow, observe how they do and how the garden looks as a whole. Later, you can always move some to a new location if you wish, and add more and different plants as you see fit. Building a rock garden is a great way to express your creativity!

Here are some popular rock garden plants. You should find most of these in your local garden center, or you could even order them online.

Small Plants	**Larger Plants**
Alyssum	Lavender
Aubrieta (purple rock cress)	Yarrow
Candytuft	Yucca
Blue Fescue	Columbine
Creeping Thyme	Black-eyed Susan
Wood Spurge	Perennial Salvias
Ajuga	Shasta Daisy
Creeping Phlox	Moonbeam Coreopsis
Poached Egg Plant	
Pasque Flower	
Alpine Strawberry	
Saxifrage	
Reticulated Iris	
Houseleeks	

A rock garden can be a source of enjoyment for the whole family, and once planted will require little in the way of maintenance: just the odd bit of weeding and maybe pruning back the more vigorous species. Creating a rock garden is a great way to invest a few hours you would otherwise have wasted watching TV!

#93 LEARN TO CODE

Budget: $$$ Time: 🕐🕐🕐🕐🕐

You don't have to be a wannabe programmer to learn to code (though a knowledge of coding will do you no harm in the jobs market). It can provide a fascinating and enjoyable challenge, and give you a better understanding of how so much modern technology operates.

Learning to code has many other benefits too. It can improve your ability to think creatively, reason logically, and work collaboratively with other people. These skills are valued by employers in many fields, and can be beneficial in your personal life as well. Little wonder more and more children are being taught to code in schools.

Coding Languages

There's no shortage of options where coding is concerned. The main possibilities include:

HTML – HTML stands for Hypertext Markup Language. It is the basic language in which web pages are written. HTML is often studied together with CSS or Cascading Style Sheets. These are used to specify how websites should be displayed in browsers.

JavaScript – JavaScript is one of the most popular programming languages. It is used to create interactive apps and websites.

Python – Python is a general purpose, high-level programming language. It is recognized as one of the easiest languages to learn, and is often the first one taught to new students on coding courses.

Ruby – Ruby is another popular, high-level programming language, which is also reckoned to be easy to learn. In conjunction with the Rails framework ('Ruby on Rails'), it has been used by large companies to build popular web applications such as Twitter, Groupon and Hulu.

Where to Learn

There are lots of websites offering free lessons in coding. Four such sites are listed below. Note that all but W3Schools require you to register by providing an e-mail address and password.

Code Academy – www.codeacademy.com/learn
At Code Academy you can take courses in HTML/CSS, JavaScript, Python, Ruby and other programming languages. Lessons take the form of interactive tutorials that let you test your new-found skills and provide tips if you make a mistake.

The Khan Academy – www.khanacademy.org/computing/cs
The Khan Academy is famous for its comprehensive video tutorials. Rather than focus on one particular language, their course uses JavaScript to illustrate concepts that apply to coding in general, while also teaching some practical JavaScript skills.

Learn Street – www.learnstreet.com
Learn Street offers online courses in Ruby (12 lessons), Python (9 lessons) and JavaScript (7 lessons). All include practical exercises for students to complete and instructional videos to watch.

W3Schools – www.w3schools.com
At W3Schools you can complete free courses in HTML/CSS and JavaScript, as well as so-called server-side languages such as SQL, PHP and ASP. The lessons are at a somewhat slower pace than those of the other three providers, so this site may be a good starting point for less confident learners.

Alternatively, you can of course sign up for classes at local colleges, which may be good for those who prefer to study with an instructor and fellow students. Whether you hope to design the next Angry Birds app or simply want to give your brain a little workout, learning to code gives you the opportunity to achieve this. So why not turn off the TV and switch the computer on instead!

#94 PAINT A ROOM

Budget: $$$ Time: 🕐🕐🕐🕐🕐

Here's a fun DIY job anyone can tackle and all the family can get involved. Painting can bring fresh life to tired, over-familiar parts of your home – and it's quicker and easier than you may think too.

The main things you will need are (of course) paint, a paint roller, and brushes for filling in corners and awkward areas. Masking tape is highly recommended to ensure you produce clean, straight edges. You will also need some old sheets or such like to protect the floor from paint splashes.

Once you've assembled all the paint and equipment you need, here's an easy six-step guide to painting a room:

1. Clean and prepare the walls

Remove dust, dirt, and grease spots with water, a little mild dishwashing detergent, and a cellulose sponge. Rinse the walls with clean water to remove the soap residue.

2. Tape the trim, window, and doorframes

Be sure to use painter's blue tape, which can be applied up to a week beforehand. Remove the tape immediately after painting, so you don't peel off any paint with it.

3. Prime the walls

It's a common myth that walls that have been painted before don't need priming. In fact, primer helps maximize the sheen and coverage of paint and provides a more uniform appearance. If you're painting a new wall or one that was previously painted a dark color, primer is essential.

4. Brush where you can't roll

Brush on paint around the trim and in the corners of walls, where your roller can't reach, with a two-inch angled brush. Extend out two to three inches from windows, doors, and moldings.

5. Use a roller to quickly paint large areas

For maximum efficiency, start at a corner of a wall and roll in a three-by-three zig-zag pattern, then fill this in without lifting the roller. Continue in sections until you're finished, painting one wall at a time.

6. Paint the trim

When the walls are completely dry, tape where the trim meets the wall. Paint the moldings and the doors and window-frames with a two-inch angled brush. A white gloss paint is the usual choice for woodwork, and again it's best to use primer as well.

More Tips

• If you're painting the ceiling too, use a roller with an extension handle. This is quicker and safer than balancing on steps.

• If you want the room to have a calm, relaxing atmosphere, use cool, pastel colors such as blues and greens. If you want something more energetic and exciting, go for warm colors like yellows and oranges. Ceilings are normally best painted white.

• If you're not sure what color will be best for your room, buy small tester pots and paint a small area with each to see how they look (in both natural and artificial light). You'll paint over these patches later, of course.

• Ensure the color(s) you use blend well with your curtains and other soft furnishings.

When it's all done, sit back, enjoy a well-earned drink, and admire your newly-decorated room. Then start planning which room you're going to paint next!

#95 TRY YOUR HAND AT
ORIGAMI

Budget: $$$ Time: ◐◐○○○

Origami is the traditional Japanese art of paper folding, which dates back to at least the 17th century. In the last hundred years it has become popular across the world and evolved into a modern art form.

The aim of origami is to transform a single flat sheet of paper into a finished sculpture through folding and sculpting techniques. The use of cuts or glue is not considered 'proper' origami. It's easy to learn the basics of origami, and there are literally hundreds of designs you can make.

It's possible to buy special origami paper, but you can use any sort as long as it will take a fold. This means that origami can be a very inexpensive hobby!

Newcomers are usually advised to start by learning the basic folds. These include the mountain fold, the pleat fold, the reverse fold, the crimp fold, and the sink fold. You can learn these from books on origami or websites such as origami-instructions.com. Once you have understood and mastered the basic folds, you can use them to create any origami sculpture you like.

The origami-instructions.com website also lists hundreds of origami designs, all with step-by-step instructions and photographs (and often videos too). Here are links to some of their most popular tutorials:

Crane – www.origami-instructions.com/origami-crane.html
Boat – www.origami-instructions.com/origami-boat.html
Cowboy Hat –www.origami-instructions.com/origami-cowboy-hat.html
Windmill – www.origami-instructions.com/origami-windmill.html
Cat – www.origami-instructions.com/origami-cat.html
Lily – www.origami-instructions.com/origami-lily.html

A popular variation is creating origami with dollar bills (or other currencies). This can make a good conversation piece in bars and restaurants, or you could impress your waiter by turning his tip into a crane! Needless to say, the origami-instructions.com website mentioned above has instructions on dollar bill origami as well.

<u>More Tips</u>

• There are many free instructional videos on the YouTube website. Do a search on Origami and see what comes up.

• Take the trouble to master the basic folds first, rather than leaping straight into model making. Understanding these folds makes origami creation far easier.

• Every crease needs to be flattened well for a successful sculpture (unless of course the instructions say otherwise). You can reinforce a crease by running the side of your thumbnail along the fold, or use a plastic ruler.

• Be patient. Origami is a contemplative and relaxed activity. If you attempt to dash through it, you're more likely to make mistakes. When starting out especially, allow yourself plenty of time, and enjoy the process as well as the end result.

• Remember you can use origami to make practical objects too. It's great for creating unusual gift boxes, for example.

• You can also use your creations as inexpensive decorations (in which case you may want to use brightly colored paper).

Many people find origami a great way of relaxing and reducing stress, and it will amuse and brighten the lives of others who see your creations as well. All you need to get started is a sheet of paper, so why not grab one now and get folding!

#96 TRACE YOUR ANCESTORS

Budget: $$$ Time: 🕐🕐🕐🕐🕐

Which of us isn't fascinated by our family history? And who doesn't secretly hope that buried somewhere in our past is someone famous or infamous?

In recent years, with the aid of the internet, it's become far easier to research your family tree. So why not take a little time to learn more about your ancestors – whose genes you carry – and find out if a royal prince or famous artist was among them?

Your first step will be to speak to members of your family, especially the older generation. Take some time to interview them, asking about brothers and sisters, uncles and aunts, and so on. You could unearth some surprising facts about your family while doing this, and with the aid of what you learn will be able to start compiling your family tree.

There are various software products and websites that will let you create a family tree and share it with your family and friends. Many allow you to add photos as well. One free online tool you can use is FamilyEcho.com.

Once you have gleaned as much as possible from your relatives, you will want to dig a bit deeper with the aid of the internet. The most popular genealogy research website is Ancestry.com. They have separate sites serving the United States, Canada, United Kingdom, Australia, Mexico and several other nations.

Ancestry.com isn't free, but they do offer a 14-day free trial, allowing you unlimited access to over a billion names. If you like what you see, they offer a variety of monthly and annual subscriptions.

Once you have entered the information you have compiled already on the Ancestry.com site, it will search through billions of historical records, photos, and other members' family trees for additional information about your family. When the software finds something, a green leaf is shown, and you can click on this to review the details.

Ancestry.com is not the only genealogy website, of course. Here are some other free resources that may be helpful in your research.

• WorldConnect Rootsweb – a world-wide online research database – http://wc.rootsweb.ancestry.com

• Interment.net – free cemetery records online – http://interment.net

• Family Search – a free research tool from the Church of Jesus Christ of Latter-Day Saints – https://familysearch.org

• 1901 Census for England and Wales – a comprehensive index to over 32 million individuals who lived in England and Wales in 1901 – www.1901censusonline.com

Many other free and low-cost research resources are listed at http://genealogy.about.com.

As you trace your family further back, you may find you need to look beyond the net for information. This could involve visiting other parts of the country, or even the world, where your ancestors once lived. You might find the information you need in church records, town halls, libraries, newspaper archives, military museums, and so on. With determined detective work, you may be able to trace your family back over several hundred years.

Don't forget to share what you learn with other family members, especially any intriguing facts you discover about your ancestors. You might also want to research any especially colorful characters in a bit more depth. Don't be too surprised if an initial quest to learn about your family history turns into an absorbing, life-long hobby!

#97 VISIT A HISTORIC SITE

Budget: $$$ Time: ◔◔◔◔◔

Wherever you live, there are likely to be dozens of historic sites you could visit on a day trip. The options include monuments, churches, historic houses and gardens, museums, national parks, old battlefields and cemeteries, and many more. Visiting these places can be both enjoyable and educational, and it is usually inexpensive (or free) as well.

To find out what's in your area, search online for 'historic sites' plus the name of your state, city or region. Many attractions have their own websites, so use these to find out more about the history of the place, along with travel directions, opening times, admission fees, and so on. Many historic sites offer discounts for children and senior citizens, as well as family groups.

There are also membership organizations for those interested in visiting (and supporting) historic sites. In the United Kingdom, the National Trust (www.nationaltrust.org.uk) looks after hundreds of historic houses, gardens, mills, forests, islands, castles, nature reserves, and even whole villages. Members get free entry to most of these attractions, along with a magazine, members' handbook, regional newsletters, and more.

There are similar membership-based heritage organizations in many other countries, including Canada (www.heritagecanada.org), Australia (www. nationaltrust.org.au) and New Zealand (http://www.heritage.org.nz). Members of these organizations often qualify for reciprocal benefits with equivalent organizations in other countries.

In the United States, the National Trust for Historic Preservation is a privately funded non-profit organization working to save America's historic places. Members receive a subscription to their quarterly Preservation magazine, discounts at over 500 historic places worldwide (including all National Trust historic sites in America), and 10 percent off the best available rates at Historic Hotels of America. You can find out more at www.preservationnation.org.

More Tips

• Check beforehand to see if there are any special events going on at the site you plan to visit. You may wish to arrange your visit to coincide with such events, or alternatively to avoid them if you would rather just see the site itself.

• Some historic sites can be quite hard to find. Check the travel instructions on the website carefully, and phone them if in any doubt. A satellite navigation system (satnav) can be a great asset as well!

• Consider booking a guided tour. This can be a great way to learn more about the history of the place in question, and you can follow up by exploring on your own.

• If taking children, check to ensure that there will be enough to keep them occupied. Many places have treasure hunts and discovery trails aimed at younger visitors in particular.

• At large sites, don't rush around trying to see everything. Take your time and schedule regular breaks, especially if with children. You can always come back to see the rest another time.

• Check whether refreshments are sold, and take a picnic meal if not. You might prefer to do this anyway, as the range and quality of food on offer at historic sites can be variable.

Enjoy your visit, and start planning another one soon!

#98 PUT UP SOME SHELVES

Budget: $$$ Time: 🕐🕐🕐🕐🕐

One thing almost any home can benefit from is more shelves. They will free up space and provide handy storage for books and ornaments. Shelves can also make an attractive contribution to a room's decor.

Putting up shelves is an easy task you can do in the time you would otherwise spend watching an episode of your favorite soap. But it's important to do it correctly, to avoid ending up with crooked shelves or shelves that fall off the wall, taking your valued possessions with them.

Here's an easy, step-by-step guide to putting up shelves correctly on walls made of drywall (also called plasterboard):

1. Assemble the tools and equipment you will need. As well as your shelf and shelf brackets, you will require an electric drill, two-inch wood screws, a pencil with an eraser, a hammer and nail for marking up, and a stud detector. You will also need a spirit level.

2. Using the stud detector, find the upright stud closest to where you want your shelves, and mark the edges with two vertical lines using a pencil. A stud is the wood framing that comprises the inner structure of the walls. It's essential to find a stud when putting up shelves, as shelves drilled into drywall are likely to collapse.

3. Mark holes for the first bracket. Take one of the shelf brackets and hold it up over the stud at the correct height. Use the spirit level to set it vertical and then mark through the holes with a pencil to show where you need to drill. Add a cross and nail dent to each mark, for more accurate drilling.

4. Drill a two-inch hole into the stud. Screw in two-inch wood screws so that the bracket fits tightly.   Repeat this for the other studs and any other shelves, using your level to ensure the brackets are correctly aligned.

5. Put the shelf in place and fix it with screws, if required. Depending on your bracket design, the shelf may need to be fixed on to the bracket, or it may just balance on the top.

6. Check the level again. If you have done this correctly, your shelf should be perfectly level.

More Tips

• If you don't have a stud finder, you can find studs fairly accurately by knocking on the wall until you hear a solid sound instead of a hollow sound.

• If fixing a shelf to a brick or masonry wall, follow the steps above, but you won't need to worry about studs. You will, however, need to use plastic wall plugs to ensure the screws are secure. Drill holes to the correct size and depth for the plugs, using a masonry drill bit instead of a wood bit.

• Screw all brackets into place before putting on the shelves. If any of the brackets are misaligned, it will be easier to fix them if you haven't already installed the shelves.

• Don't put more weight on your shelves than is recommended for the type of wood and the method of installation.

• The general method set out above applies equally when putting up a shelving system with long vertical brackets.

#99 LEARN A NEW RECIPE

Budget: $$$ **Time: 🕐🕐🕐🕐🕐**

It's easy to get into a rut cooking the same old dishes, week in, week out. So why not turn off the telly and spend a little time learning a new recipe (or two) instead?

A good place to start is your current recipe books, especially any you haven't opened for a while. Go through them carefully, looking for any interesting-sounding recipes you might like to try. An added benefit is that you are quite likely to rediscover old favorites that have slipped out of your repertoire for some reason. Now could be the perfect time to bring them back!

Another good source of recipe ideas can be friends and family (parents and grandparents especially). If you enjoy something they have cooked, make a point of asking for the recipe. Or you could simply explain that you are looking for new ideas and ask if they have any good recipes they could share. The chances are they will be flattered by the implied compliment regarding their cooking skills!

Still another idea is to host a recipe party. Invite a few like-minded friends to bring some food they have cooked, along with the recipes they used. This obviously works best with foods that can be prepared in advance, but you can allow guests to add the finishing touches in your kitchen. Not only will you learn some new recipes, you'll get to taste the food as well!

Finally, a great, free resource for learning new recipes is, of course, the internet. One of the best-known sites is Allrecipes.com. This has many thousands of recipes in categories including appetizer, main dish, dessert, breakfast/brunch, healthy, slow cooker, and vegetarian. As well as the recipes, you can see comments from people who have tried them along with any variations they suggest. Users can also rate recipes from one to five stars, which gives you a quick way of zeroing in on the most popular ones.

Another useful feature of Allrecipes is that you can search by ingredient. It lets you look for dishes including up to four different ingredients, which is great if you have a glut of produce from your garden or just leftovers to use up! You can also exclude up to four ingredients if you or a family member dislike them or are allergic to them. Finally, you can also specify what meal the recipe should be for, the dish type, and even how long it should take to prepare.

There are many other recipe sites as well, of course. Three others well worth checking out are listed below.

BBC Food – www.bbc.co.uk/food

The BBC Food website has over 13,000 recipes, including many by celebrity chefs from TV shows.

Recipe – www.recipe.com (this easy-to-remember site features over 20,000 recipes, with links to discount coupons from local supermarkets).

My Recipes – www.myrecipes.com

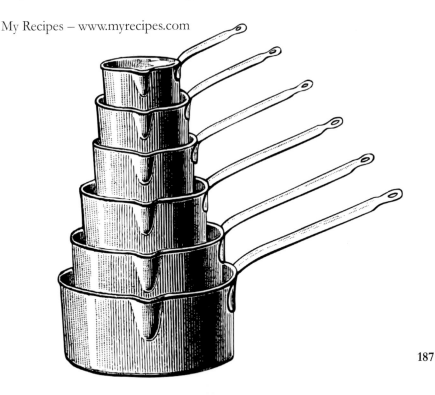

#100 PLAY A DICE GAME

Budget: $$$ Time: 🕐🕐🕐🕐🕐

Almost every home has a few dice knocking around, or you can buy them cheaply from stationery stores. Add a pen and paper, and you have all you need to keep your family and friends amused for hours!

Here are a few popular dice games to get you started:

Beetle

Beetle is a traditional British party game for two or more players. You'll need a single die and a pen and paper for each player.

The aim is to be first to draw a complete beetle. Players take turns to throw the die and draw a part according to the number thrown. Traditionally, the rolls are as follows:

6 is for the body (one)
5 is for the head (one)
4 is for the tail (one)
3 is for a leg (six)
2 is for an antenna (two)
1 is for an eye (two)

A player must roll a 6 for the body before any other part may be drawn. To the body one may attach the head, legs or tail, but the head must precede the antenna and eyes. The first to draw all the required parts in the required numbers shouts 'Beetle' and is the winner!

Big Six

This classic game for two to six players dates back to medieval times. You'll need a single die, plus some playing chips or tokens. You'll also need to draw a board with six spaces numbered one to six. Players start with five chips each, and the aim is to be first to lose them all.

Players take turns to roll the die. If the corresponding space on the board is empty, put a chip there; but if there's already a chip there, you must take it. If you roll a six, you always put one of your chips on space number six, regardless of how many chips are there already. Chips on this space are out of the game and never picked up again.

The first player to get rid of all their chips is the winner.

Stuck in the Mud

This is a game for two to six players. You will need five dice and a pen and paper for keeping score.

The aim is to achieve the highest score, but you can only score on a roll that doesn't include the numbers 2 and 5. Any dice which show a 2 or a 5 become 'stuck in the mud'.

The first player rolls all five dice. If they have rolled any 2s or 5s, they don't score any points for this throw. If they haven't rolled any 2s or 5s, add up the total of the dice and remember it.

The same player then throws again, but only with dice that didn't roll 2s and 5s before. Again, if they roll any 2s or 5s they fail to score. Throws without 2s and 5s are added to their previous total.

The player continues this way until all their dice are 'stuck'. At this point they write down their total, and pass the dice to the next player.

After five rounds the player with the highest score is the winner.

#101 TAKE A FREE ONLINE COURSE

Budget: $$$ Time: 🕐🕑🕒🕓🕔

If too much TV is causing your brain to atrophy, why not bring it back to life by signing up for a free online course?

Many universities and other institutions world-wide now offer short courses free of charge online. Whatever subject may interest you, the chances are there will be a free course on which you can learn the basics (at least). Alternatively, why not simply browse the thousands of courses on offer and see what catches your eye? This can be a great way to broaden your horizons and discover new interests.

One good place to start is the UK-based Futurelearn.com. This site is owned by the Open University, an organization with over forty years' experience delivering distance learning. Their free online courses are run in partnership with over twenty British and international universities, together with other educational and cultural institutions such as the British Library and the British Museum.

Courses can be studied online in a few hours a week and typically last from three to ten weeks. They consist of a combination of video lectures, articles, discussions, quizzes, and other activities. As well as studying the course materials and completing assignments, students are encouraged to interact with one another and discuss the course and any issues it raises on social media.

Recent Futurelearn courses have included Begin Programming with Java, The Science of Medicines, Shakespeare and His World, Exploring Our Oceans, The Secret Power of Brands, and Discover Dentistry. All courses are free to anyone, anywhere in the world.

Another valuable resource for finding free online courses is the Open Education Database at http://oedb.org/open. This lists over 10,000 free online courses offered by institutions including Oxford University, the Massachusetts Institute of Technology and The University of Michigan. You can browse courses by category, including arts, business, education, engineering and computer science, health and medical, liberal arts, math and science. Note that while some of these courses are tutor-led and run on specific dates, others simply consist of downloadable self-study material.

Finally, Coursera at www.coursera.org is another site listing free online courses with universities and other institutions worldwide. Courses featured here have included a six-week course in songwriting from Berklee Music College in Boston, an eight-week introduction to forensic science from Nanyang Technological University in Singapore, and an eight-week course on learning to teach online from the University of New South Wales in Australia.

•Free online courses don't usually lead to a qualification, though you may get a statement of accomplishment or similar. In a few cases you may be able to take an examination for the award of a diploma or certificate, though a fee may be charged for this. These short courses are mainly for personal interest rather than career development, though there is nothing to stop you applying for more advanced training – to degree level and beyond – if you really become engrossed by a subject!